Florian Schreiner

Content management and protection using Trusted Computing and MPEG-21

Florian Schreiner

Content management and protection using Trusted Computing and MPEG-21

Concepts for metadata, protection and implementation

Südwestdeutscher Verlag für Hochschulschriften

Impressum / Imprint
Bibliografische Information der Deutschen Nationalbibliothek: Die Deutsche Nationalbibliothek verzeichnet diese Publikation in der Deutschen Nationalbibliografie; detaillierte bibliografische Daten sind im Internet über http://dnb.d-nb.de abrufbar.
Alle in diesem Buch genannten Marken und Produktnamen unterliegen warenzeichen-, marken- oder patentrechtlichem Schutz bzw. sind Warenzeichen oder eingetragene Warenzeichen der jeweiligen Inhaber. Die Wiedergabe von Marken, Produktnamen, Gebrauchsnamen, Handelsnamen, Warenbezeichnungen u.s.w. in diesem Werk berechtigt auch ohne besondere Kennzeichnung nicht zu der Annahme, dass solche Namen im Sinne der Warenzeichen- und Markenschutzgesetzgebung als frei zu betrachten wären und daher von jedermann benutzt werden dürften.

Bibliographic information published by the Deutsche Nationalbibliothek: The Deutsche Nationalbibliothek lists this publication in the Deutsche Nationalbibliografie; detailed bibliographic data are available in the Internet at http://dnb.d-nb.de.
Any brand names and product names mentioned in this book are subject to trademark, brand or patent protection and are trademarks or registered trademarks of their respective holders. The use of brand names, product names, common names, trade names, product descriptions etc. even without a particular marking in this works is in no way to be construed to mean that such names may be regarded as unrestricted in respect of trademark and brand protection legislation and could thus be used by anyone.

Coverbild / Cover image: www.ingimage.com

Verlag / Publisher:
Südwestdeutscher Verlag für Hochschulschriften
ist ein Imprint der / is a trademark of
AV Akademikerverlag GmbH & Co. KG
Heinrich-Böcking-Str. 6-8, 66121 Saarbrücken, Deutschland / Germany
Email: info@svh-verlag.de

Herstellung: siehe letzte Seite /
Printed at: see last page
ISBN: 978-3-8381-2785-9

Zugl. / Approved by: München, Technische Universität München, Diss., 2010

Copyright © 2011 AV Akademikerverlag GmbH & Co. KG
Alle Rechte vorbehalten. / All rights reserved. Saarbrücken 2011

Acknowledgments

This book and the presented research have been elaborated at the Technische Universität München in the Institute for Data Processing, which was an inspiring and procreative environment for my research.

Firstly, I would like to thank my supervisor Prof. Dr.-Ing. Klaus Diepold for his outstanding assistance and support during the work at the institute. I am grateful for the inspiring and motivating discussions, which helped me in the research and development. Furthermore, I want to thank him for the comments and the review of this book, which were a valuable support in its preparation.

I'm also thankful for the great opportunity to work with international partners and colleagues by participating in the standardization of the MPEG group and the collaboration within the OpenTC project. Both organizations and their participants had a remarkable impact on my research and the development of my personal and professional experience.

Furthermore, I am very grateful for my colleagues in the Institute for Data Processing, who assisted with valuable advice and support in the various tasks and challenges in the research and education.

Finally, I would like to thank my parents, family and friends for their outstanding support and understanding in the work as a researcher and the elaboration of this book.

Munich, Germany   Florian Schreiner
August 2011.

Abstract

Content management systems are widely used for the collaborative creation, description, exchange and protection of digital content. This book presents several improvements in content management systems using the MPEG-21 standards and the Trusted Computing technology. The book can be divided in three parts: content sharing, protection mechanisms and implementation.

The content sharing is improved in the area of free distributable and open content. There is already an impressive amount of free distributable content available, e.g. user-created content, but distribution, sharing and reuse of the content is hindered by incompatibilities in format and a lack of metadata. The goal of this book is to identify commonalities for open content and to specify a format to enhance the sharing and reuse of this type of content. The resulting format is mainly based on the MPEG-21 standards, which specify an interoperable framework for the delivery and management of digital media. The proposed format consists of a file format with integrated metadata, which is attached to each content to communicate its major information and properties. An important aspect of the metadata is the licensing of the content and the management of these licenses. The proposed concepts enable the assignment of licenses to unambiguously communicate the licensing of the content with an enhanced user experience. The resulting format enables an automatic processing and indexing of content to enhance the license management and sharing of free distributable content.

The second part of the book deals with protection mechanisms in the content management using the Trusted Computing technology in the MPEG-21 standards. The MPEG-21 standards do not define a concrete concept for security mechanisms and have no specific support for Trusted Computing. This part of the book presents three methods for the application of Trusted

Computing in MPEG-21 to protect content. The first method shows the required extensions of the MPEG-21 standards to support Trusted Computing in a decentralized architecture. The second method presents a concept to integrate qualified timestamps based on Trusted Computing in digital signatures. The third method concludes this part with an enhanced concept for authentication within the OpenID system.

The final part of the book presents a prototypical implementation, which demonstrates the presented concepts and shows their feasibility. All concepts are integrated into a working content management system, which implements several functions to enhance the distribution and the protection of content.

Contents

1 Introduction   1
    1.1 Overview of content management 2
    1.2 Existing systems and requirements 4
    1.3 Problem statement 5
    1.4 Overview of the contributions 7

2 Metadata for sharing content   9
    2.1 Fundamentals 9
       2.1.1 Free distributable content 11
       2.1.2 Extensible Markup Language 12
       2.1.3 MPEG standards 12
       2.1.4 MPEG-7 Multimedia Description Schemes 13
       2.1.5 MPEG-21 14
          2.1.5.1 Digital Item Declaration (DID) 14
          2.1.5.2 Digital Item Identification (DII) 15
          2.1.5.3 Rights Expression Language (REL) 16
          2.1.5.4 File Format 18
          2.1.5.5 Event Reporting 19
       2.1.6 MPEG-A 20
    2.2 Problem statement 21
    2.3 Comparison with other systems 24

	2.3.1	MPEG-21 based systems	24
		2.3.1.1 Axmedis framework	25
		2.3.1.2 Digital Media Project	25
	2.3.2	Applications of Creative Commons licenses	27
		2.3.2.1 Creative Commons Rights Expression Language	27
		2.3.2.2 Open Mobile Alliance	28
2.4	Metadata and file format specification		29
	2.4.1	Concept	30
	2.4.2	Components	31
		2.4.2.1 Technology selection and file format	32
		2.4.2.2 Content identification	34
		2.4.2.3 Legal licenses and author information	35
		2.4.2.4 Rights expressions	37
		2.4.2.5 License representation	39
		2.4.2.6 Content rendering	41
		2.4.2.7 Adaptation and aggregation	41
		2.4.2.8 Feedback mechanism	44
		2.4.2.9 File Format	46
		2.4.2.10 Cryptographic signatures	47
	2.4.3	Summary and outlook	47

3 Protection using Trusted Computing   49

3.1	Fundamentals		49
	3.1.1	Encrypted data in XML	50
	3.1.2	MPEG-21 IPMP	51
	3.1.3	Digital signatures in XML	52
		3.1.3.1 Qualified timestamp	53
		3.1.3.2 XML Advanced Electronic Signatures	55

	3.1.4	Trusted Computing		56
		3.1.4.1	Trusted Platform Module (TPM)	57
		3.1.4.2	Secure storage	57
		3.1.4.3	Integrity measurements	58
		3.1.4.4	Internal keys and certificates	58
		3.1.4.5	Attestation Identity Keys and PrivacyCA	59
		3.1.4.6	Timestamping	60
		3.1.4.7	Tick counter	60
		3.1.4.8	Tickstamp	61
		3.1.4.9	Timestamp Protocol	62
		3.1.4.10	TCG Software Stack	64
	3.1.5	Web based authentication with OpenID		65
		3.1.5.1	Web-based Single Sign On	65
		3.1.5.2	OpenID	65
3.2	Problem statement			69
	3.2.1	Secure content storage and transmission		70
	3.2.2	Timestamps in digital signatures		71
	3.2.3	User authentication		72
3.3	Comparison with other systems			73
	3.3.1	Concepts for secure content exchange		74
		3.3.1.1	SmartRM system	74
		3.3.1.2	Key management in MPEG-21 IPMP	75
		3.3.1.3	Other proposals	76
	3.3.2	Timestamps in digital signatures		77
		3.3.2.1	Applications of tickstamps	78
		3.3.2.2	Representation of timestamps	78
	3.3.3	User authentication		79
		3.3.3.1	VeriSign's OpenID SeatBelt Plug-in	79

		3.3.3.2	Other proposals	80
3.4	Developed concepts			81
	3.4.1	Secure content storage and transmission			81
		3.4.1.1	Digital signatures	82
		3.4.1.2	Content storage	83
		3.4.1.3	Transmission of content	85
		3.4.1.4	Distribution and addressing of users	90
		3.4.1.5	Summary	92
	3.4.2	Timestamps in digital signatures			92
		3.4.2.1	GenericTimeStampExtensionType	93
		3.4.2.2	TPMTimeStampType	94
		3.4.2.3	Tickstamp	95
		3.4.2.4	Verification of the timestamp	96
		3.4.2.5	Integration of the TPM-timestamp in signatures	97
		3.4.2.6	Example	98
		3.4.2.7	Summary	99
	3.4.3	User authentication			100
		3.4.3.1	Overview	100
		3.4.3.2	Components	101
		3.4.3.3	Use cases	103
		3.4.3.4	Registration	104
		3.4.3.5	Authentication	107
		3.4.3.6	Deregistration	109
		3.4.3.7	Evaluation	110
		3.4.3.8	Summary	111
	3.4.4	Summary of the concepts			111

4 Implementation   **112**

    4.1   Application scenarios 112

    4.2   Architecture 113

    4.3   Components 115

            4.3.1   TPM Module and TSS 115

            4.3.2   Content Management Application 116

                    4.3.2.1   Architecture 116

                    4.3.2.2   Functionalities 118

                    4.3.2.3   Cryptographic operations 120

                    4.3.2.4   Timestamps 121

            4.3.3   Content Server 124

                    4.3.3.1   Metadata 124

                    4.3.3.2   User Authentication 126

                    4.3.3.3   Key management 127

            4.3.4   Browser add-on 127

                    4.3.4.1   Architecture 128

                    4.3.4.2   Functionalities 129

            4.3.5   OpenID Provider 132

                    4.3.5.1   Registration 132

                    4.3.5.2   Authentication 133

                    4.3.5.3   Deregistration 134

    4.4   Summary 134

5 Conclusion   **135**

Chapter 1

Introduction

The management of digital content plays an important role in modern society. Content refers to all types of digital data that can be consumed by another user, like videos or music, but also presentations or documents. Nowadays, more and more content is created, and as a consequence, the demand for distribution and sharing of content increases with the permanent progress in communication and network technologies. There is already an enormous amount and variety of content available and the amount is increasing permanently.

Content is created by all parts of the society such as industry, organizations or users. In industry, there are several domains generating content, which is then shared and distributed either to other companies or users. Examples are movies, documents within companies or commercials created by the film industry. Organizations like political parties or academic institutions also create content, which is then distributed or even promoted to the public.

Furthermore, the content created by users gains in importance as more and more users are equipped with a communication device or a mobile camera. The content created with these devices is then shared with social websites that enable the user to easily share the content with everyone, friends or other groups of users. This change in society additionally contributes to the steady increase of shared content. This content is also advantageous as it is a rich source of valuable content, which can be reused for other purposes.

Nevertheless, the overwhelming amount is obstructive and problematic, because it is unmanageable for a single user and the discovery of a specific content is a difficult task. Content management in general tries to solve this problem as it provides methods and technologies to enhance the collection, managing and publication of content regardless of its type. This book proposes improvements for the management of content to ease the sharing and distribution of content. Security is also very relevant with regard to the content, which could be, for example, confidential documents or private information. This book also presents several methods for the protection of such content within content management systems.

1.1 Overview of content management

Content management has a wide scope and there are a large number of systems and applications available. To enable the efficient management of content, metadata is required, which describes the content and enables e.g. the indexing or an efficient processing of the content. Metadata is additional information, which is attached to content to describe it in a specified format. The metadata can be categorized in two different types of formats: binary- or text-based formats.

This book focuses on the management of digital content using text-based metadata conforming to the Extensible Markup Language (XML) [41] standard. XML specifies the syntax of machine-readable documents to express the required information with a set of hierarchically structured elements. The semantic of these elements is not specified in the XML specification, but there are several standards defining such semantics with a focus on a specific application domain. An example for such a standard is the Dublin Core Metadata Initiative (DCMI), which defines the terms for such elements in [10]. Another organization is the MPEG group, which specified in MPEG-7 [86] a comprehensive set of elements for the description of multimedia content.

Another aspect of content management is Digital Rights Management (DRM), which are systems describing and controlling the rights associated with content. DRM systems are categorized in Enterprise Rights Management systems and Multimedia Rights Management systems. Enterprise Rights Management systems manage the distribution and, in particular, the usage of the content. Their goal is to protect confidential documents and to ensure that the granted rights are respected. These systems are limited to

1.1. OVERVIEW OF CONTENT MANAGEMENT

operate within a particular environment, for example to manage documents within a company or to handle the exchange of documents between multiple companies. They can be configured to fit the requirements of the company and can represent working flows of documents within the company. Examples of Enterprise Rights Management systems are Adobe LiveCycle Rights Management [1] and Oracle Information Rights Management [25].

In contrast to this, Multimedia Rights Management systems are not limited to a particular environment. They manage the distribution of multimedia content, which is usually distributed to all users who are allowed to consume the content. The support of other multimedia systems is, however, a critical issue, because many of the existing Multimedia Rights Management systems are not compatible with each other, which prevents the unhindered exchange of content. There are some organizations, that have developed an interoperable Multimedia Rights Management system to overcome this limitation. One example is the Open Mobile Alliance (OMA) [21], which has developed a system mainly for the mobile phone industry and wireless communication networks. There are many other systems in this domain, but most of them are small initiatives with a very limited scope. Another significant organization is the MPEG group, which developed the comprehensive MPEG-21 framework to enable the interoperable sharing and delivery of content. The concepts presented in this book are based on the MPEG-21 framework, because it supports a wider range of application domains than the other systems. Since the transition from Multimedia Rights Management systems to Enterprise Rights Management systems is fluent, the presented concepts in this book can be generally applied for Multimedia Rights Management systems as well as Enterprise Rights Management systems.

Another aspect of content management is the protection of confidential content, which requires a security basis for the key infrastructure. Most of the existing DRM systems use "obscurity" or smart cards as the basis of security. Obscurity means that a secret software algorithm is applied, which hides the key in the client to hinder the user from accessing the content. This is an economic solution as it does not require additional hardware and it is also supported in legacy systems. The security of this method is, however, only very limited, as the user can obtain the key easily, when he discovers the algorithm used for the obfuscation. An example for such a system is the Windows DRM system [16] or the FairPlay system [4]. More security is provided by smart cards, which are secure cryptographic devices capable of storing keys securely. They have the disadvantage that there are many types of smart cards and each type requires specific hardware and drivers. To overcome this disadvantage the Trusted Computing Group (TCG) [29] developed the specification of the Trusted Platform Module (TPM) [103], which is basically a smart card with a standardized interface and capabilities. Furthermore, the TPM is by default built into many platforms so that no additional secure hardware is required in the client. For this reason, the TPM is used in this book as a security basis for content management and several concepts are presented to enhance the protection of content.

1.2 Existing systems and requirements

There are a high number of systems available which enable the management and protection of content. Most of the systems differ inherently from the concepts and the systems described in this book, because they have different properties and requirements.

A number of systems are proprietary and they do not provide any specifications or descriptions of their architecture. One reason is that many systems use obscurity as their security basis. In order to prevent users from circumventing this security mechanism, the architecture and the functionalities of these systems are kept secret. Another reason is the business model of the companies, which want to prevent competitors in the market realizing systems or devices with similar functionalities. This would decrease their influence in the market. As a result, the file format and the embedded metadata are proprietary and thus incompatible with other systems or devices, which would provide similar functionalities. This lack of interoperability hinders the exchange and usage of content. Therefore, this book deals with specifications and standards which are published with the aim to achieve interoperability.

There are a couple of systems whose specifications are published, like the afore mentioned system from the Open Mobile Alliance (OMA) [21]. These systems, however, are usually limited to a specific domain. They also do not provide efficient functionalities for the license management or support for Trusted Computing technologies. In contrast to that, the MPEG-21

1.3. PROBLEM STATEMENT

framework is broad in scope and supports a wide range of application domains and functionalities. There are other systems based on MPEG-21, which require a thorough evaluation. This evaluation is presented in section 2.3.1.

Another aspect is that the focus of most content management systems is the centralized enforcement of rights and usage constraints on the content. The authors or publisher of content primarily want to ensure that only the granted rights are allowed, which restricts the user in the usage of the content. The aim of the software is to enforce these usage constraints. The aim of this book is to achieve a decentralized system, which ensures only confidentiality and integrity of the content. The user is not limited in the usage of content; however, the adherence of the rights remains still in his responsibility.

The security basis is another aspect in content management. Generally, the security basis is not defined in the specifications of the majority of the DRM systems and its realization depends on many factors like the business model or the application domain. The Trusted Computing Group specifies the TPM as an interoperable and secure device, but its functionalities are not exploited in current content management systems. The aim is to use some functions of the TPM in content management to enhance the security of these systems. A description of the relevant functions and the differences to existing concepts is shown in section 3.3.

1.3 Problem statement

The developed concepts in this book focus on free distributable content and the goal is to improve its management and sharing. Free distributable content is the content that can be shared without costs. It can be of any type, which makes it difficult to manage, as there is no common format or generalized information within the files. Nevertheless, the content has some information in common, which is currently stored apart from the content. The identified common information consists of the license information, intentions of the license, relationships between adapted content, and reference to the author.

The concept in this book overcomes this problem by specifying a superior file and metadata format, which enables the attachment of common information directly to the content. To develop such a format, it has to be defined what license information is required and how this license information can be adequately integrated into the file format. Furthermore, the intentions of the licenses should be converted to a machine-readable representation, which enables the automatic processing to assist the user in the management of the content. This enables for example the software to notify the user, if it detects that he intends to perform an action which might infringe the license. In particular, the adaptation and aggregation of content are two challenging actions, which require further investigation to realize assisting functionalities for the user.

Another aspect for free distributable content is the reference to the author, which needs to be investigated. A clear reference is required to express the attribution of the content to the author and to inform about important events of his content. It has to be determined how this reference can be realized and which additional functionalities are required to inform the author.

Furthermore, the development of protection mechanisms for content relevant to security is another important aspect in this book. The aim is to ensure authenticity, integrity, verifiability and confidentiality of content. The Trusted Computing technology provides a security basis to achieve a protection with these properties. A key management architecture has to be defined, which enables the encryption and signing of content. Furthermore, qualified timestamps from the TPM prove the existence of a content at a specific point in time. It has to be shown how these timestamps with their special structure can be supported and integrated into the existing standards. The key management and the timestamps also require modifications to the MPEG-21 framework and an optimal method for their integration needs to be elaborated.

Another aspect is the user management, which is required for the protected exchange of content. To ensure authenticity of users, the OpenID system is combined with the Trusted Computing technology. The book proposes a concept of how the functionalities of the TPM can be applied within the OpenID system to enhance the authentication mechanism.

1.4 Overview of the contributions

This book presents a system which enhances the management and the protection of content in several aspects. The management of free distributable content is improved with a specialized file format and a selected set of metadata, which enhances the sharing and reuse of content. The metadata contains the information, which is common to the free distributable content. The developed improvements provide the following properties:

- Open file format based on standardized technologies
- Support for any content independent of its type
- Enhanced license information and specification
- Embedding of author and creation information
- Assisted adaptation and aggregation
- Feedback mechanism

These properties are realized on the basis of the MPEG-21 framework, which are selected and combined to create a concise solution for free distributable content. The details of these functionalities and their representation in MPEG-21 is presented in section 2.4.2.

Another aspect is the protection of content, which is achieved with the application of the Trusted Computing technology within the MPEG-21 standards. To protect the storage and exchange of confidential content, the key management functionalities of the TPM are integrated into the MPEG-21 standards. This enables a secure and interoperable exchange of the protected content. Furthermore, a concept is presented to integrate timestamps created by the TPM into signatures. This enables the ability to prove the existence of a content at a specific point in time. Another concept investigates the authenticity of the user for the content management and applies the OpenID authentication system to verify the identity of users using the Trusted Computing technology.

Finally, a prototypical implementation of a content management system is presented, which contains realizations of all presented concepts combined in a single system. The implementation applies the MPEG-21 standards and the Trusted Computing technology for the management and the protection of content.

This book is organized as follows: chapter 2 introduces and describes the concepts to enhance the sharing of content. After that, chapter 3 presents the methods for the protection of content using Trusted Computing. Finally, chapter 4 presents the implementation of the previous concepts.

Chapter 2

Metadata for sharing content

The publication and the sharing of content is an important aspect of modern society. It fosters the exchange of information, interaction between people and collaboration to achieve complex goals. The amount of shared content increases permanently. The steady advancement of the Internet also increases this demand and the exchange of content will gain more and more in importance. In this chapter, different aspects of content and different ways of publication are presented. The deficiencies in the current content sharing lead to a set of requirements that allow the improvement and simplification of the current state. A system is proposed that can overcome these limitations.

2.1 Fundamentals

In this book, the term "author" represents the creator of the content and the term "user" is any person, which has access to the content within the system. The term "content" is used for data, information or knowledge within the electronic communication domain. Metadata for content is an important aspect, because it has significant impact on the management of content. This is shown in examples for the two options of content exchange: centralized services or decentralized files.

The exchange of content with a centralized service uses a common party that stores, indexes and presents the content to the user. The user can browse the content and eventually view, edit or retrieve it. This option is used in web content management systems, where the content is stored in a repository, and a software presents the content via a web server to the user. The content in the repository is indexed and usually also enriched with additional information to enhance the searching and browsing of the repository. The user profits from this metadata, but a disadvantage is that for any operation, the user requires a connection to the service. When the user downloads the content from the service, he generally cannot use the metadata anymore, because the repository uses a proprietary format and the metadata cannot be retrieved from the repository without efforts.

A decentralized transmission of content, for example from user to user, generally uses files for the transportation and the exchange. Such a file can either contain a single content like a video file or multiple content like an archiving file. These files are transferred to the recipient, which are called consumer in the rest of the book. The consumer directly receives the content and he can use the content without a connection to the provider. Generally, however, the consumer does not receive any information about the author or the licensing of this content, because the files do not contain metadata with this information. A potential solution can be, for example, the embedding of a license in an archive as a separate file, but the relation between the license and the content also gets lost when the content is extracted from the archive. Metadata is thus an important factor, because it is required in many situations, but the integration and interoperability of the metadata has to be improved.

One part of metadata is the specification of the intellectual property of the content. The intellectual property is usually described in a license, which contains terms from the author defining how the content may be used. A license consists of three parts: the licenser, the licensee and the terms of the license. The licenser is the party who holds the rights on the content, e.g. the author. The licensee can be a person, organization or everybody. The license terms describe the granted rights of the licenser to the licensee.

There are many different types of licenses e.g. licenses for software or contracts between specific parties. A special form of license is used when the licensee allows the free distribution of the content. The next section introduces free distributable content and its licensing to show the properties for this type of publication.

2.1. FUNDAMENTALS

2.1.1 Free distributable content

Free distributable content is defined as content that can be perceived and distributed for free. Many of the free distributable content is "open content". This content was created by authors who want to share the content with the public and want to enable its reuse. The author grants a permission like the free distribution or the reuse within a specific type of license, also called an open content license. In this license, the author can specify in a legal way how other people may use the content.

It exists already a remarkably high volume of open content, and the amount of new content increases steadily. Open content comes from a general movement to openness and reuse that can be found in many different domains. One well-known example is the open source movement which evolved together with the components of the operating system Linux. Most components of Linux are published as open source code using a license certified by the Open Source Initiative [22]. These open source licenses were designed for the application on source code. In contrast to that, the open content movement is not limited to source code. It is more general, because open content can be any creative work independent of the type or the domain. In particular, the distribution and availability of content in the multimedia domain is growing rapidly. Examples of such repositories with open content are sharing websites like the Wikimedia Commons [31]. In April 2010, this repository already contained over 6.4 million media files [32], which shows the success and importance of open content.

The license of this content is a central aspect, because with this license the published content can be automatically shared and reused. Several organizations have developed concrete licenses for this purpose. One wide-spread organization providing this type of licenses is Creative Commons [9]. Some of their licenses are also compatible to the common GNU licenses, which shows the importance and generality of the licenses defined by Creative Commons. Each of these licenses has different properties, which allows the author to choose the license with the adequate properties he wants to apply. Some of these licenses fulfill the criteria of open content and allow the sharing and reuse of the content. Other licenses contain more restrictive constraints, for example they do not allow the reuse of the content.

Licenses that do not allow the reuse are often applied when the content contains information that is in a final state and should not be adapted. One movement using these licenses is the "Open Access" initiative. Open Access fosters the open publication and exchange of public-funded research results. These results are available to the public for review and to foster the technological progress, but the content may not be adapted for example. The impact of Open Access in science can be seen in the Open Access Declaration [6], which was developed and signed by 255 world-wide scientific institutions and organizations in 2003.

These and other organizations promote and support free distributable content. There are, however, several problems hindering its exchange and distribution. One example is content sharing websites, where content using a specific license can be searched and browsed on the web interface. Nevertheless, once the content is downloaded, the license is no longer attached to the content, or only the human readable license text is embedded within the content. The content cannot be automatically organized or searched without the manual recreation of an index. This increases the effort for the organization and management of content between different systems. In this book, this and other problems are solved by using the technologies and standards developed by the MPEG group. The next sections give an introduction to these technologies and standards.

2.1.2 Extensible Markup Language

The Extensible Markup Language (XML) [41] is a basic standard, which allows information to be declared and structured in a text based format. The standard was specified by the World Wide Web Consortium (W3C) and is used in several international standards for the structuring of information. XML is a machine-readable format, which can be processed and implemented effortless. It is wide-spread in many applications and thus a good basis for interoperable standards.

2.1.3 MPEG standards

The MPEG group is a working group of the ISO/IEC association, which consists of the International Organization for Standardization (ISO) and the

2.1. FUNDAMENTALS 13

International Electrotechnical Commission (IEC). The MPEG group is responsible for the standardization in the coded representation of digital audio and video and related data. The developed standards have a high impact in the multimedia sector and already many devices apply MPEG standards for the representation of multimedia content.

Among other standards, the MPEG group has developed the MPEG-7 and the MPEG-21 framework, which are sets of standards for the interoperable use of content between different systems. Furthermore, the MPEG-group has specified the MPEG-A standards, which integrate other standards in application specific formats. The next section presents a specific part of MPEG-7, which is relevant in this book. After that, the other mentioned MPEG standards are explained.

2.1.4 MPEG-7 Multimedia Description Schemes

MPEG-7 [86, 87] specifies a set of standards for the representation of metadata, which describes multimedia content. This metadata can be used for example for the management, the creation, the consumption, the governance and the organization of content as well as for the representation of user information. One standard of MPEG-7 defines a binary representation of this metadata, while the other standards use XML as their basic format. The specified metadata describes information about the content, independent of its type. The MPEG-7 standards support thus a wide range of application domains and foster the interoperability of multimedia content.

One part of MPEG-7 is the Multimedia Description Schemes standard [64, 94], which is also known as ISO/IEC 15938-5. It defines an elaborated system of XML schemes for the description of content. The standard specifies the syntax of several schemes, descriptors and their databases. One part of the standard is the scheme for media description, which represents information for the creation, the production or the usage of content. The creation of content is described with a descriptor in the scheme: "CreationDescriptionType". It contains information about the content like the title, the license or the creator.

This is a short introduction to MPEG-7, which explains the basic information for the following sections. The next section introduces similarly the relevant standards of MPEG-21.

2.1.5 MPEG-21

MPEG-21 is a framework of standards for the consumption and distribution of multimedia content [46, 45, 68]. It supports trading of content as well as rights and protection mechanisms, adaptation and reporting. The MPEG-21 standards can be understood as a set of tools, which need to be combined to realize a comprehensive solution for a specific application domain. The standards are independent of the type of content, as they specify generic methods for the description and processing of data. They specify an interoperable infrastructure for the creation, the consumption and the distribution of content.

The MPEG-21 standards are also a basis for the development of DRM systems, because they define basic tools for such systems. In the past, the term Digital Rights Management was misused for the enforcement of business interests in certain market segments, which led to an incompatibility of current systems. MPEG-21 tries to overcome these limitations with a generic and interoperable framework, which can serve as a basis for the development of compatible systems for the management of content. The MPEG-21 standards are thus a good basis for DRM systems, which have the focus on the interoperability between different implementations or application scenarios. For this reason, the MPEG-21 framework was chosen as an important set of tools for the development of the presented concepts in this book.

The MPEG-21 standards introduce the term "Digital Item" as a superior structure of content. It packages the metadata in a single element to enable the description, the structuring, the identification and the referencing of content. The Digital Items are the fundamental objects in the whole MPEG-21 framework. Their definition and processing in MPEG-21 is explained in the following sections.

2.1.5.1 Digital Item Declaration (DID)

The MPEG-21 part 2 specifies the Digital Item Declaration (DID) [70, 44] using the identifier ISO/IEC 21000-2. It defines the term Digital Item as 'a structured digital object with a standard representation, identification and metadata within the MPEG-21 framework'. A Digital Item comprises the content and all metadata in a single re-identifiable package. The standard

2.1. FUNDAMENTALS

defines the structure of the Digital Items and the semantic of the elements in the structure. For this purpose, the standard uses XML schemes and specifies the syntax and the semantic of the XML elements. Within the DID, the content is called resource, which can be either embedded directly or referenced with a link into the Digital Item.

Furthermore, the DID standard defines the Digital Item Declaration Language, which is the fundamental structure for the delivery in the MPEG-21 framework. The language allows an aggregation of several Digital Items or sub-items within a Digital Item to be created. This provides the possibility to combine several Digital Items in one DID document and to structure them within the document. A DID document is the highest level of the structure, which is usually associated with a file or a media stream. An example of such a file is a music album. The album is a Digital Item, which is the highest level in the file. The album contains several sub-items, which represent the tracks of the album.

The Digital Item itself is structured in several elements allowing the embedding of additional metadata or content in the Digital Item, or for these to be attached. The structure supports for example the embedding of supplementary metadata about the content or the insertion of an additional content to increase the user experience.

The Digital Item Declaration Language also allows to insert a content in different versions in a Digital Item. These versions can then be distinguished with choices, which show the differences between the versions. It can be used, for example, to let the user decide which version of the content should be presented. These mechanisms offer a high range of flexibility and enables the usage of the standard in a wide scope of application scenarios.

In the rest of the book the capitalized term "Digital Item" or "Item" refers to the definition according to the DID. The lowercased term "item" is used with the general meaning in English.

2.1.5.2 Digital Item Identification (DII)

The identification of the Items is specified in the MPEG-21 part 3, the Digital Item Identification (DII) standard [71]. This standard has the ISO number ISO/IEC 21000-3 and defines the usage of identifiers on the basis of

16   CHAPTER 2. METADATA FOR SHARING CONTENT

the Uniform Resource Identifiers (URI) standard [39]. It allows the assignation of unique and persistent identifiers to the Items and resources within the MPEG-21 framework. These identifiers are independent of the type of content and can be structured hierarchically. The DII standard does not define a new scheme for identification of Items or resources. It specifies the method by which new or existing identification schemes can be categorized and embedded into an Item. Examples of existing identification schemes are the International Standard Book Number (ISBN) [57] and the International Standard Recording Code (ISRC) [58]. Both schemes are compatible with the method of identification in the DII standard and can thus be applied to an Item.

Furthermore, the MPEG group introduced relationships between Items in the Amendment 1 [72] of the DII standard. These relationships allow to relate the Items to each other and to specify the type of this relationship. Other Items are referenced within an Item using their unique identifier. Each Item may have multiple relationships to other Items. The type of each relationship is defined in the MPEG-21 Rights Data Dictionary standard, which specifies nine different types of relationship. These types declare, for example, that an Item is a component of another Item or that an Item is an adaptation of another Item.

2.1.5.3 Rights Expression Language (REL)

The MPEG-21 Part 5 specifies the Rights Expression Language (REL) [74, 107] which is also called ISO/IEC 21000-5. The REL is a versatile and a flexible language, which expresses the granted rights over a content, also called rights expressions. For this purpose, the REL defines the syntax and the semantic of an interoperable license, which declares these rights expressions in XML. Such a license is very flexible and can express a wide range of functionalities. Examples of these functionalities are distribution licenses, offer licenses, delegation of licenses or revocation of licenses. These functionalities go beyond the scope of this book and will not be explained more in detail.

A license of the REL contains several rights expressions, which express the rights that are granted to a principal on a selected content from an issuer under defined conditions. The issuer is an entity, which holds the rights and grants them to other users. The principal is an entity, which is the target

2.1. FUNDAMENTALS 17

of the rights expressions, i.e. the rights are granted to the principal. The principal can be specified in several variants, which allow users as well as devices to be specified.

The elements of the REL can be classified in core elements, standard extension, multimedia extension and profiles. The core elements contain essential elements of the REL, which are required for the basic functionalities. These elements include the basic license structure or the variants of the principal. The standard extension defines elements, which are not essential in the REL, but still beneficial in many application domains. Examples of these elements are the declaration of payment for the consumption or restrictions regarding the territory of the user.

The multimedia extension specifies the syntax and the semantic of the elements, which can be applied to multimedia content. These elements enable, for example, the marking of multimedia content. This part also includes the rights for the consumption of multimedia content, which are for example play, print or adapt. These rights are adopted as a reference from the MPEG-21 Rights Data Dictionary (RDD) [76] standard. This standard defines these rights in a hierarchical structure to consistently define their semantic meaning. The rights are related to each other in an ontology, which can be interpreted by humans and are also machine-readable. This enables the definition of a clear, concise, coherent, integrated and unique set of terms for the application in the REL.

The last class of elements in the REL are the profiles. Profiles specify basically a subset of the previous elements, which are required in a specific application domain. The result is a concise and balanced set of elements, which fulfills the needs of the specific application domain. The reduced complexity of the profiles reduces the efforts for the implementation and provides interoperability. An implementation conforms to a profile if it implements the profile completely. Every implementation which conforms to the profile is thus compatible to another implementation, as both understand the elements in the profile. As a result, the profiles serve as conformance points for the implementation and foster the interoperability. As stated before, profiles are mainly subsets of existing elements, but they can also introduce new elements if they are required in the application domain. This flexibility allows the definition of a profile as a complete and comprehensive solution for the respective application domain. The REL has three profiles at the time of writing: the MAM (Mobile And optical Media) profile, the DAC (Dissemination And Capture) profile and the OAC (Open Access Content) profile. The MAM profile and the DAC profile will not be explained further in this book, because they are profiles for specific application domains, which are not relevant for this book. The OAC profile will be explained in detail in section 2.4.2.4.

Besides the semantics and the syntax of the elements, the REL defines an authorization model, which describes the processing and interpretation of a license in an implementation. It is required when a user wants to perform a given action and the implementation has to determine whether the user is authorized for that action. For example, a user wants to play an Item, which is an audio recording. When the user triggers the action 'play', the implementation has to check whether the right to play is granted to the current user. For this reason, the implementation evaluates the rights expressions within the license of the respective Item. The standard specifies the method for this evaluation in a mathematical way to obtain identical results on different implementations. The detailed method is not explained in this book and can be looked up in the MPEG-21 REL standard.

There are other Rights Expression Languages from other organizations available, which can be also abbreviated as REL. Within this work the term REL refers only to the MPEG-21 Rights Expression Language unless otherwise noted.

2.1.5.4 File Format

Part 9 of the MPEG-21 framework specifies the MPEG-21 File Format and has the identifier ISO/IEC 21000-9 [78]. It is object-oriented and extends the ISO File Format to support the MPEG-21 framework and the delivery of Items. The file format serves as a container for the DID and the Items within it. The DID is mandatory in the standard. Furthermore, the format can contain all or some of the content, which belongs to the Item. The File Format enables thus the packaging of the metadata and the content into a single object. This eases the delivery, the distribution and the adaptation of Items.

A file conforming to the MPEG-21 File Format uses an own identifier, which allows to recognize a file conforming to the standard. The format

2.1. FUNDAMENTALS

is divided into boxes, which contain the metadata and the content. The standard specifies the structure of these boxes and the information stored within them. Furthermore, the orientation on the ISO File Format enables a flexible processing of the format. If required, the format can be created as a MPEG-21 file as well as a MPEG-4 file. An implementation can thus read the same file as a MPEG-4 file or as a MPEG-21 file depending on the compatibility with the application. The support of MPEG-4 enables the usage of the format with legacy applications and eases the transition for these applications to the XML based MPEG-21 format.

2.1.5.5 Event Reporting

The MPEG-21 part 15 is called Event Reporting and is identified with ISO/IEC 21000-15 [69, 101]. This standard specifies the creation and management of events in the MPEG-21 framework. An event can be understood as an action on an Item or as an interaction with an Item, which triggers the creation and transmission of a report. The standard specifies the method of requesting a report to an event, the creation of the report and its transmission. The reports enable the tracking of content, which a provider can use to have an insight about the distribution and usage of the content.

To insert a request for a report on a certain event the Event Reporting standard specifies the Event Report Request. The Event Report Request can be either embedded as metadata into an Item or transmitted as a standalone Digital Item. It informs the receiving implementation that a report should be created on the selected event. If an Item contains such an Event Report Request, the implementation starts to monitor the occurring events and triggers the creation of a report on the requested event. The created report is called Event Report in the standard.

For the creation of an Event Report, the implementation uses the information of the Event Report Request to assemble the required information. For that purpose the Event Report Request specifies which information will be inserted into the report, to whom the report will be transmitted and the method of transmission. The information in the report is specified generically to support all possible types of information and metadata. This enables the selection of any metadata within an Item and for this information to be transmitted to the provider of the content. After the creation of the Event

Report, it is transmitted to the given recipient with the respective method of transmission.

The structure and semantic of an Event Report is also specified in the standard to achieve an interoperable creation and interpretation between different implementations. An Event Report can also be transmitted to several recipients, which enables the notification of many parties at the same time. Furthermore, Event Report Requests can also be embedded in Event Reports, which enables an ongoing processing of the reports. If a recipient receives such an Event Report, the embedded Event Report Request can request the recipient to take further action. This can be, for example, the acknowledgment of the reception or the forwarding of the report to another party.

This is the last standard from the MPEG-21 framework, which is introduced. The next section presents the MPEG-A standards, which partly use the MPEG-21 framework as building blocks.

2.1.6 MPEG-A

MPEG-A is relevant to this book as some of the developed concepts were adopted and standardized by MPEG within MPEG-A. This section introduces MPEG-A briefly.

The standards in MPEG-A are identified with the number ISO/IEC 23000 and have the name Application Formats (AF). They specify interoperable formats for the interchange, management and presentation of media for particular application scenarios. The standards can also be seen as "superformats" [48], which combine and integrate required technologies into a comprehensive and single solution. These technologies are the building blocks of the AFs and they can be either MPEG standards or specifications from other organizations.

Each Application Format supports a limited set of application scenarios and on the basis of these application scenarios the required MPEG standards or supplemental technologies are chosen. These building blocks can be either included entirely or only necessary parts can be selected. The content within the AFs is not limited to multimedia content. It can be of any type if it is required by the application scenario. The resulting Application Format is

2.2. PROBLEM STATEMENT

thus a concise set of selected technologies that are aligned to each other and that specifies an optimized solution for the predefined application scenarios.

This section concludes the fundamentals for this part of the book. The next section presents the problems which are investigated in this book.

2.2 Problem statement

The exchange and reuse of content plays an important role for the open content and open access movement. There are, however, several problems hindering the sharing, management and reuse of this content. The free distributable content as described in section 2.1.1 has much information in common, but the different types of content in the respective domains hinder the efficient processing and exchange. The information that the content has in common is the legal license, the intentions of the license and the reference to the author.

The legal license text contains a juridical text that is written to express precisely the granted rights on the content. Many legal licenses have been developed for the publication of free distributable content, e.g. the already mentioned Creative Commons licenses. These licenses are available for free and they can be applied to any content. The license text is then the effective basis for the decision-making of a court on licensing conflicts between two parties. The court interprets the license and decides on these issues using the laws of the country. That is why most licenses are provided in multiple versions to reflect the different laws in the respective countries and also to consider the consecutive changes in the law and judicature over time. A system, which is capable of managing these licenses and their versions should be able to precisely identify the license used and requires a global identification scheme. With this identification, the systems can create indexes that allow the user to search or browse for specific licenses. Furthermore, it should be possible to attach the legal license text directly to the content, so that every consumer can directly access and view the license used at the time of publication. It is also necessary for some licenses to publish the license text together with the content to be legally valid, e.g. the Mozilla Public License [19]. Furthermore, a URL to a website with some information about the legal license can assist the consumer to determine if the content is suitable.

There is a wide spectrum of legal licenses with an enormous variety in conditions and properties. These licenses can be characterized with a small amount of principal properties, which appear in most of the licenses. Creative Commons determined these principal properties and defined a set of licenses according to these properties. Thus, the licenses defined by Creative Commons can represent a wide range of the existing license spectrum. In this book, these licenses are examined in detail and applied substitutional for most of the other existing licenses.

Another aspect is the automated processing and interpretation of the license. This has several advantages, which can be seen in an example for open source software. Currently, the license of the source code is added as an extra file or directly embedded in the source code. Neither method allows to automatically determine and process the license, because every license has its unique text and the text has to be searched everywhere in the source code, which is very complex. This problem is even more complex in big software projects, which consist of several components, which are licensed differently. This makes it difficult to determine the correct license for the whole project. The compatibility of all licenses has to be checked to determine which properties the resulting license must have. It is in the interest of the author to find out the correct license to avoid legal dispute subsequently. If a piece of software is able to interpret the license, it can assist the user to determine the correct license and to respect all licenses from the components. This interpretation cannot be performed on the license text directly, because the text can only be interpreted by a human being. The text has to be converted to a machine-readable language, which a program can interpret and process. A method for the conversion has to be defined and the capabilities of this mapping have to be examined. Furthermore, the machine-readable license is only a representation of the legal license, which the software can use in different ways to assist the user. The different possibilities of utilization have to be determined and discussed.

Many licenses want to foster the sharing and reuse of content; however, some restrictions must still be respected. A common restriction is that the content should have a permanent attribution to the author declaring who is the rights owner and the licensor. This information is currently either individually embedded in the content itself or only loosely connected to the content. Additionally in the case of adaption or aggregation of content, the

2.2. PROBLEM STATEMENT

author of the original content has to be referenced. This is typically also a requirement in the license that the adapted content should reference the original content to specify its source. For these use cases, a solution has to be found that allows to respect these restrictions and to fulfill the requirements of the license.

Furthermore, an author may wish to receive some feedback about the usage of the content even after the publication. The feedback is a notification on certain usage of the content, which is sent to the author. The received notifications could be used to determine, for example, the distribution or the popularity of the content. For this purpose, the structure of this notification, the triggering event and the transferred data have to be specified as well as the method of transportation has to be investigated.

Furthermore, a global identification of the content is required. On the one hand, to be able to recognize a specific content, on the other hand, to unambiguously reference other content for the feedback, the adaptation and the aggregation. An identification scheme has to be chosen, which is scalable and which supports a hierarchical management of the identifiers using multiple coordinating authorities.

All this information needs to be bundled with the content into a package for the release. To support the exchange and the sharing of the package, the transportation in a file is the straightforward solution. The format of the file has to be specified in detail. There are a large number of existing file formats, which are potential candidates. The optimal format has to be found regarding the complexity of integration and interoperability to the existing formats. The format should also be extensible to allow an evolution in the future development.

The MPEG group has developed several standards for the coding and the representation of multimedia and other data, which are widely deployed and accepted in the market. The MPEG-21 framework is one example where the MPEG group has specified a powerful set of standards that can fulfill many needs for the interoperable usage of content between different systems and devices. Each standard in MPEG-21 was developed for a specific functionality, which is fulfilled as comprehensively as possible to allow a wide application of the standard. Although the standard provides a solution for the demands of the market, this wide approach hinders the application of the standard, because the integration and implementation of the standards require a large effort in the development. For particular application domains only a minimal and concise set of technologies is required to create an adequate solution. This is the concept of the MPEG-A standards, which contain specifications that are limited to particular application scenarios. A MPEG-A standard selects and combines parts of other standards in a concise specification that can be adopted and implemented. This selection and combination of standards was performed as part of this work. It has to be executed precisely to achieve a minimal and optimal basis for interoperability in the application domain.

2.3 Comparison with other systems

This section presents a comparison to related systems which share some commonalities with the presented work in this book. There are a large number of existing systems, which manage content using licenses. In particular, the wide distribution of open content and its licenses increases the number of relevant systems significantly. To limit the comparison, only systems based on the MPEG-21 standards or the Creative Commons licenses are considered.

2.3.1 MPEG-21 based systems

The application scope of the MPEG-21 framework is very wide as it provides technologies applicable in many different domains. One principal domain is DRM, which defines a system to govern and protect the usage and the distribution of content. In the past, the term was frequently used for the governance of multimedia content as a mechanism for copy protection. This created a negative impression in the perception of these systems. These are, however, not directly related to the technology and mechanisms required for the implementation of Digital Rights Management systems. Many systems for Digital Rights Management of multimedia content were developed and are available in the market. However, the majority of the systems are closed source and their specification is not publicly available. They can thus not be examined for the application of MPEG-21 technologies, which is required to determine their relevance for this book. For this reason, this book presents and compares only the systems whose specifications are publicly available and can be compared to the concepts of this book.

2.3. COMPARISON WITH OTHER SYSTEMS

2.3.1.1 Axmedis framework

One system based on MPEG-21 is the AXMEDIS framework [5], which is the abbreviation for "Automating Production of Cross Media Content for Multichannel Distribution". It is a comprehensive framework for business dealing with content management and it provides a solution for several platforms and channels along the whole value chain. AXMEDIS supports a large number of business models and deals with the production, the management, the protection and the distribution of content.

For the protection and the rights management, it is based on the MPEG-21 framework and uses the MPEG-21 REL standard to specify the licenses for the content. It also uses the MPEG-21 Event Reporting for the statistical surveillance of the content. The AXMEDIS framework concentrates on business models and content protection for distributors with a variety of functionalities. It focuses on the business to business or business to customer distribution and the control of the distribution of the content. This is required as the content has a value, which should be protected.

This is in contrast to the concept of this book, which enhances and eases the distribution of the content using MPEG-21. The content is available for free and a restriction of the distribution is counterproductive. The AXMEDIS framework thus has a different focus in the content management and the application of the technologies of the MPEG-21 framework. This is also perceivable in the license management. AXMEDIS concentrates on the creation, the processing and the enforcement of the rights expressions in the licenses and provides mechanisms for the expression of contracts. The focus in this book is the representation of licenses for free distributable content like the ones from Creative Commons using MPEG-21 technologies. AXMEDIS has no support for such licenses or mechanisms for their management.

2.3.1.2 Digital Media Project

The Digital Media Project (DMP) [11] is an organization that consists of several universities and companies. Their goal is to develop specifications and software for the promotion of Digital Media to the consumer while the rights of the owner should be respected. The DMP published the specification of the Interoperable Digital Rights Management Platform [13], which is still under development in cooperation with the MPEG group. Several parts of the specification were contributed to MPEG, which were standardized for example in the Media Streaming Application Format or the MPEG-21 REL DAC profile. The specification is developed further with the specification of the MPEG Extensible Middleware (MXM) and the Advanced IPTV Terminal (AIT) standards in the MPEG group.

The Interoperable Digital Rights Management Platform is implemented in the Chillout software, which is also the reference software of the specification. The specification and the software are based considerably on the technologies in MPEG-21 to realize a majority of the functionalities. Some functionalities not supported by MPEG-21 are realized by own developments in the DMP project. The resulting software consists of several independent devices, which have a clear predefined task and communicate with each other using a defined set of protocols. The DMP project also adopted the developed MPEG-21 OAC profile in the Chillout software, which enables the representation of Creative Commons license. This functionality is included to increase the scope of the software and is considered as a form of lightweight DRM in the whole concept of the specification.

The DMP project has a strong focus on the protection of the rights of the creator or the rights holder. It supports a number of use cases, which are required in the classical understanding of DRM systems for multimedia content, for example home domains. A home domain allows a consumer to use a specific content in a set of devices, which he or she declared beforehand as his property. The specification supports a sizable set of rights, which enable a detailed declaration and enforcement of rights on the content. Furthermore, the DMP project developed several elaborated protocols and messages, which are required for the implementation of heterogeneous devices in different levels of the value chain from the creation, the distribution to the consumption of content. This differs from the focus in this book, which concentrates on the declaration of rights as information to the consumer and not on the enforcement of these rights. The representation of the Creative Commons licenses is integral to the concepts in this book. The DMP project also does not specify details about the enforcement of the rights like cryptographic concepts, which are required to ensure the correct interpretation and processing of the rights. The following chapter of this book describes such cryptographic concepts, but with the focus on the protection of the content

2.3. COMPARISON WITH OTHER SYSTEMS   27

and not the enforcement of the rights.

2.3.2 Applications of Creative Commons licenses

Other initiatives and organizations enhance the content and license management of free distributable content. As this book concentrates on the representation of the licenses defined by Creative Commons, this section presents other similar projects which apply these licenses. Although these projects use other technologies than MPEG-21, they differ to the presented concepts of this book.

2.3.2.1 Creative Commons Rights Expression Language

Creative Commons specifies and publishes its licenses in three different formats: a human readable license deed, the legal license text and a machine readable code. The human readable license deed is a simplified presentation of the license, which is easily and quickly understandable for the end-user. The legal license text is the license, which is legally valid and written as a juridical text. The machine readable code is a representation of the license, which is investigated more in detail.

The machine readable code is defined as the Creative Commons Rights Expression Language (ccREL) [36], which specifies descriptive metadata to represent the licenses from Creative Commons in a machine-readable Rights Expression Language. It has the goal to enable the automatic processing and interpretation of the license of a content for search engines and other applications. The ccREL is specified in the Resource Description Framework (RDF) [83] and the Extensible Metadata Platform (XMP) [34]. Both standards describe methods to formalize information in a machine readable format, which is compatible to the HTML technology of the Internet. The ccREL allows the licenses to be identified and for a reference to a chosen license to be clearly declared. Furthermore, the four main properties of the licenses can be declared, which are similar to the description of the human readable license deed. A license declaration, conforming to the ccREL specification, is attached as additional information to the content, which can be interpreted by applications understanding the format.

Creative Commons developed implementations which are capable of parsing and presenting such metadata. One implementation is a plug-in for the Mozilla-based applications, which detects a ccREL license and presents an icon in the status bar of the application to indicate the presence of a Creative Commons license. Another implementation is a basic editor for the creation and the modification of a license declaration conform to the ccREL.

The ccREL specifies a declarative method of representation, which enables the identification and the assignment of the licenses to content. It does, however, not contain information about the interpretation and the processing of the machine readable code. For example, it does not contain information about how the license should be presented or at what point in time. It is up to the application to process and to present this information to the user. This is a significant disadvantage, because the processing of the license information should be identical in different implementations to achieve interoperability and to enhance the user experience.

2.3.2.2 Open Mobile Alliance

The Open Mobile Alliance (OMA) [21] is a consortia of several companies which have developed open and interoperable standards for the mobile phone industry and the wireless communication networks. One of the specified standards is the OMA DRM Rights Expression Language (OMA REL) [88], which specifies a Rights Expression Language for the controlled consumption of Digital Content on authenticated devices. The OMA REL is based on the Open Digital Rights Language (ODRL) [20], which specifies the rights over the content similar to the MPEG-21 REL, but with a different syntax and semantic.

The ODRL also contains a support of Creative Commons licenses and integrated this support in the standard as a separate profile. It is specified as the ODRL Creative Commons Profile [55] and enables the representation of the licenses and their semantic directly as a part of the ODRL. Because of this seamless integration, the profile benefits from the automated processing and the interpretation mechanisms of the ODRL. The extensions of the ODRL Creative Commons profile can be embedded within the declaration of the ODRL at a desired point, which enables a precise choice of the method of presentation of the license. This realizes a more powerful method of expressing the licenses.

Although the ODRL provides this precise method of expression, it lacks in the detailed representation of the Creative Commons licenses. The representation orientates predominantly on the ccREL from Creative Commons, which specifies the license in native terms in a declarative form. The ODRL Creative Commons profile adopted the terms of the ccREL and included them in the specification. Thus, the specification does not define a semantic meaning of the adopted terms, which prevents the automatic interpretation of the license properties. The goal of this book is to enable this interpretation by mapping also the detailed license properties of the Creative Commons licenses to standardized terms, which can be automatically interpreted. This is achieved using the MPEG-21 framework and in particular the MPEG-21 REL.

This concludes the comparison to other systems. The next sections explain the developed concept for the management of content in detail.

2.4 Metadata and file format specification

This section presents the descriptive metadata of the developed solution. This work was contributed to the Moving Picture Experts Group (MPEG) [17], which is a working group responsible for the development of standards for coded representation of digital audio and video and related data. The MPEG group accepted the work as an International Standard with the identifier ISO/IEC 23000-7 and the full name "Information technology - Multimedia application format (MPEG-A) - Part 7: Open access application format" [80], further called Open Access Application Format. An article describing the standard was published in [97] and [96]. Within the MPEG group the work was discussed and improved in several meetings with international representatives of other countries interested in the work. The rights expressions for this standard are specified separately in ISO/IEC 21000-5/Amd3 with the name "REL OAC (Open Access Content) profile" [75]. These rights expressions were developed based on the requirements of the Open Access Application Format.

Furthermore, an implementation of the standard was developed and standardized as reference software of the Open Access Application Format as "ISO/IEC 23000-7/Amd 1 - MPEG-A - Open access application format: Conformance and reference software" [81], which is a part of the Open Access Application Format standard. The reference software for the rights expressions is published within the amendment "ISO/IEC 21000-8 Information technology - Multimedia framework (MPEG-21) - Part 8: Reference software - Amendment 1: Extra reference software" [77]. This is an optimal basis to achieve interoperability, because it allows companies and organizations the adoption of the standard for the development of software.

Some examples for the application of the standards are the publication of teasers, e-learning material or the release of public funded research results. This content can be published as public domain or an existing license can be applied, like the ones of Creative Commons. The publication and sharing of user-created content is also becoming more and more important in the web. Another example is the open source movement. The Open Access Application Format enhances the management of this content, because it enables the creation of content repositories and provides information for search engines, which can index and categorize the content.

In the following section the Open Access Application Format is explained in detail. At first the overall concept is shown as an overview and afterwards the components are explained in detail.

2.4.1 Concept

The basic flow for the content consists of three steps: the creation, the distribution and the consumption. This flow is depicted in figure 2.1.

The first step is the creation, in which the author can package his content into a single file and enrich it with metadata. The content can be any creative work the author wants to publish and share. It can be of any type, for example a presentation, a document or an audio file. The author can combine multiple and different content in the file, for example he can package presentation slides together with a recorded audio file from the respective

2.4. METADATA AND FILE FORMAT SPECIFICATION

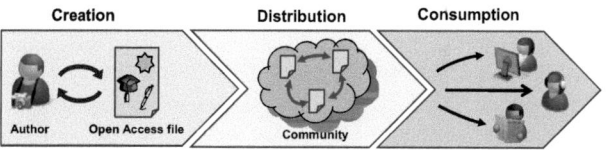

Figure 2.1: Basic scenario for the file format and metadata

speech. Additionally, the author can add metadata to the content, which describes the content as supplementary information for the consumer. In the example of a presentation, this metadata can be the contact details or a short description of the presentation. Moreover, the author can add licensing information that defines how the consumer may use the content.

When the author has finished packaging the content, he can release the file and distribute it to the public or a specific group of people. This is the second step as depicted in figure 2.1. The distributable files conform to the Open Access Application Format and they are called from now on released file. In the distribution, the attached metadata increases the visibility of the content, because it helps the consumer to easily find and to categorize the content. The consumer does not need to open the file by himself anymore to get some more information about the content. A released file also supports search engines, which can use the XML-based metadata to allow consumers to search for content that matches certain criteria, for example a specific license. This increases the spreading and enables a more efficient exchange.

In step three, the consumer has received the chosen released file and wants to view or to use the content. If the content was published with a license, the consumer is informed about the license terms and he has to agree to the conditions. This ensures that the consumer is aware of the conditions and that he knows how he is allowed to use the content. After the consumer has agreed to the license, he can consume or use the content. After this basic explanation, the details of the concept are explained in the following sections.

2.4.2 Components

The described basic conditions and functionalities of the system are realized in a new file format, which is optimized for the effective exchange and the sharing of content. This format is a minimal point of interoperability, which allows compliant applications the parsing of the file and to make the inner content available to the consumer. The embedded content has metadata assigned to it, which the application can use as information or as rules for the processing. As a summary of the previous sections, the following overall functionalities of the Open Access Application Format are:

- Open and standardized file format
- Global identification of the published content
- Legal license information
- Author and Creation information
- Machine-readable rights expressions
- Adaptation and aggregation of content
- Feedback mechanism for the author

These functionalities and their realization will be described in the following sections.

2.4.2.1 Technology selection and file format

By means of this list of functionalities the appropriate technologies are selected and adopted to realize the respective functionality. The MPEG-21 framework provides a comprehensive and interoperable basis for the realization for most of the functionalities. The set of standards in MPEG-21 were examined and restricted to the necessary elements to fulfill the respective function. Some descriptive functionalities are not provided in MPEG-21. For these cases the specific parts of MPEG-7 were chosen and integrated into the specification.

The following standards are included to specify the file format and the metadata:

- MPEG-21 Part 2 - Digital Item Declaration (DID)
- MPEG-21 Part 3 - Digital Item Identification (DII)
- MPEG-21 Part 5 - Rights Expression Language (REL)

2.4. METADATA AND FILE FORMAT SPECIFICATION

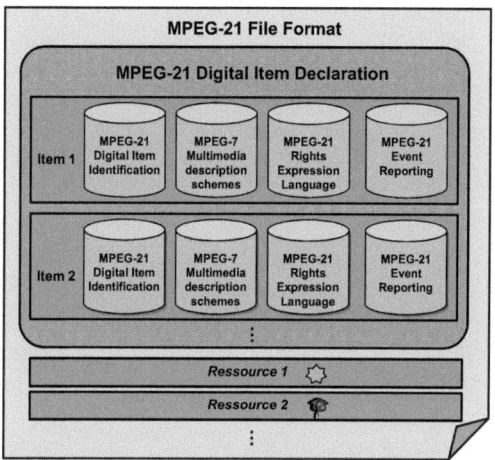

Figure 2.2: Hierarchical structure of the standards within a file

- MPEG-21 Part 9 - File Format
- MPEG-21 Part 15 - Event Reporting
- MPEG-7 Part 5 - Multimedia description schemes (MDS)

The MPEG-21 File Format provides the overall file format, which contains the content and the metadata. The other standards specify the metadata of the content. They are structured hierarchically within the file format, which is depicted in figure 2.2.

As introduced before, the content as binary data is called resource within the MPEG-21 framework. The resources are embedded at the end of the file in consecutive order. The other XML-based MPEG-21 standards specify the metadata, which describes the resources.

To complete the overview, the XML-based metadata is described briefly. The whole metadata is framed in the MPEG-21 Digital Item Declaration (DID). This standard declares the Items, which comprise the content and its associated information in a single entity. An Item contains a reference to a specific resource in the file and with this reference, the resource and the respective metadata are linked. Several Items can be added as a list into the DID, where each Item corresponds to a resource. Within the Item the MPEG-21 Digital Item Identification (DII) specifies identifiers for the Item. The MPEG-7 Multimedia description schemes are used to add descriptive information about the content and its license. A machine-readable representation of the license is modeled with the MPEG-21 Rights Expression Language (REL) [74]. The last MPEG-21 standard in the list is the MPEG-21 Event Reporting [69], which provides a feedback mechanism about the usage of the content.

Knowing the file structure and the basic relationships between the standards, the mentioned functionalities of the format will be explained in detail in the following sections.

2.4.2.2 Content identification

The identification of the content is a central aspect, because it allows the indexing and recognition of the content. The MPEG-21 Digital Item Identification (DII) specifies methods to uniquely identify Items, description schemes and the relationships to other Items or identification schemes. For this work, only the globally unique identification of Items is required. The specified identifiers are based on the Uniform Resource Identifiers (URI) standard [39]. This standard specifies a URI as a string of characters, which can identify abstract or physical resources. The syntax of this string allows a hierarchical structure with different levels. This hierarchy can be used to establish a decentralized and scalable management of the identifiers using multiple authorities for the different levels. With this scheme, globally unique identifiers are specified in which each content has its own identifier. This enables the re-identification of a content that if the identifiers of two Items are identical, the corresponding content also has to be identical.

Additionally, algorithms for locating an Item, like online resolution services are supported. One example of such a resolution service is the Domain Name System (DNS) resolution system [40]. With this service only the identifier of an Item is required to locate the Item itself. This mechanism is particularly useful for "RelatedIdentifiers" but not mandatory. RelatedIdentifiers are specified in DII and they create an unambiguous reference from one Item to another Item. The relationships between the Items can also be

2.4. METADATA AND FILE FORMAT SPECIFICATION 35

categorized, for example in an adaptation the relationships states that an Item is the adaptation of another Item. This referencing is also integrated and is explained in section 2.4.2.7.

2.4.2.3 Legal licenses and author information

The license is a central aspect of the publication, because it defines the granted permission on the usage of the content. The author can define his own license with individual conditions or he can choose a generic license, for example one of the licenses defined by Creative Commons. Generally, it has to be considered that the author can also assign multiple licenses to a single content. This is a common practice in cases where there are different groups of consumers. Such cases include different communities or specific market segments. Each license is a statement to the consumer, which informs him about the legal permissions for the usage of the content. Thus, the consumer is highly interested in the license and demands a clear notice of the license and its version. It is essential for both sides, the author and the consumer, to explicitly declare the license used.

There are three ways of license declaration in the system to satisfy this demand: as a text, a URI or a web page. The declaration as text means that the license text is included directly in the metadata. This is also often required, because the license is generally only legally binding in the textual form. Only the license text expresses precisely the granted permissions and the consumer should use this text to know the granted permissions. This is particularly important if the author uses an individual license. Therefore, the embedding of the whole license text is the general approach, although it is very inefficient, because the consumer has to read and to interpret the text carefully to determine the granted permissions.

This effort is reduced if the author uses a generic license, which the consumer possibly already knows or is easy to interpret. In this case, the consumer only requires an identifier that allows him to recognize the license. For this purpose, the URI can be used, which contains a unique identifier to declare unambiguously the exact license and version used. This identifier has to be globally unique, which can be realized similarly to the identifiers of the DII with decentralized registration authorities. An example of such a URI is "http://creativecommons.org/licenses/by/3.0/", which is the identifier of one of the licenses defined by Creative Commons.

In this example the identifier is simultaneously also a URL for a web page. At this URL the consumer can find some additional information about the license and its properties. This information can assist the consumer in understanding the license more efficiently. Other licenses, which are identified differently than with a URL, require an additional URL field to lead the consumer to a web page. This URL can be specified separately in the format to provide an independent method for the declaration of a web page with additional license information. It is specified as a related material to the content within the metadata, to express that the URL only provides further information about the license.

All three possibilities for the license declaration are realized with the MPEG-7 Multimedia description schemes (MDS) standard. It is a comprehensive standard from which only the CreationDescriptionType scheme was required and integrated into the Item as descriptive metadata. Furthermore, the CreationDescriptionType contains various descriptive data that is not essential in the application domain of the system. For that reason, the CreationDescriptionType was further restricted to a minimal set, which provides the necessary descriptive metadata.

Besides the declaration of the license, the author is also declared within this scheme. The author of a content can be either one or several persons. Several persons are required in the case, when the content is a result of a collaboration. According to that, the CreationDescriptionType allows one or multiple authors to be specified. This information is also related to the license, because it declares the issuer of the license and the attribution of the content to the author. The attribution is also part of many licenses, because it assigns the creation of the content to the author, who wants to show and to declare this association to the consumer. The author is described with the following information:

- first and last name,
- name of the organization,
- address,
- e-mail and
- web page.

2.4. METADATA AND FILE FORMAT SPECIFICATION 37

With this information, the author can be identified and also contacted. Furthermore, the CreationDescriptionType also contains information about the title of the Item, the time of its creation and the author of the content. The title contains a succinct description of the content, which an implementation can use for the presentation to the consumer. The time of creation declares the point in time, when the Item was created and published from the author.

2.4.2.4 Rights expressions

A clear license declaration is important for the author and the consumer. In section 2.4.2.3, the license identification was eased with the use of a unique identifier. This identifier, however, does not provide an automatic parsing and interpretation of the license. This can be achieved with rights expressions that allow the intentions of a license to be modeled in a machine-readable way.

The MPEG-21 Part 5 - Rights Expression Language (REL) [74] specifies a method to declare and interpret such rights expressions. A rights expression is a permission given to a Principal on a resource from an issuer under defined conditions. The semantic of these expressions and the authorization model are defined in this standard. Each permission grants a specific right, which allows a certain usage of the resource.

The REL provides a method to specify rights expressions with a specific semantic meaning in XML. The realization of these rights expressions is not defined in the REL. It is up to the application scenario to define how the rights expressions are processed and presented to the consumer. This depends on many factors, like the value of the content or the business model. For example, the rights expressions can be either enforced or alternatively only presented as a notification to the consumer. In the case of open content, it is sufficient to present the expressions to the consumer and to notify him that he might be not be allowed to perform a certain action.

To support the automated processing and interpretation of the license, only a limited set of the REL is required. Furthermore, the REL has to be extended to support some specific properties of the licenses. The resulting set was standardized as a profile in MPEG with the name OAC (Open Access Content) profile [75]. The MPEG group created a separate profile for

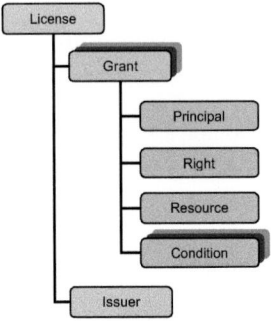

Figure 2.3: Structure of the rights expressions

this set of rights expressions, to ease the integration of the profile in other applications. One other application using the OAC profile is the MPEG-A standard Media Streaming Application Format [79].

The rights expressions can be used to provide a variety of functionalities. To have an overview about these functionalities, the basic structure and the most important XML elements are explained. The structure of the rights expressions for this work is shown in figure 2.3.

In the following paragraphs, the names of the XML elements and the attributes appear in *italic*. The *license* element is the root element for the REL. It has two child elements: *grant* and *issuer*. The *issuer* is the rights holder who created the rights expressions. The *grant* element can appear multiple times in a *license*. It specifies the permission of a *right* to a *principal* on a *resource* under specific *conditions*. The right defines the allowed action on the content and can be for example *play* or *print*. The *principal* is a person or entity, which is the target for the granted *right*. Multiple *conditions* can be added to a *grant*, to restrict the granted right in specific aspects.

The most important elements from the REL are listed in table 2.1. The underlined elements are not defined in the REL specification or any profile before the OAC profile. They are defined in the OAC profile, because they are required for the support of specific license properties.

The elements can be categorized into two different purposes: license representation and content rendering. The rights *play*, *print*, *execute* describe

2.4. METADATA AND FILE FORMAT SPECIFICATION

Table 2.1: Rights and conditions in the MPEG-21 REL OAC profile

	Elements
Rights	execute, play, print, adapt, governedAdapt, governedCopy
Conditions	copyrightNotice, nonCommercialUse, sourceCode, territory

different ways of rendering content. The other rights and conditions enable the specification of a representation of licenses. Both purposes are explained in the following sections.

2.4.2.5 License representation

The aim of the rights expressions is to provide a method to express the intentions of a license in a machine-readable and interoperable way. This would allow an automated processing of the license, which could assist the consumer in the license management. The license management is particularly important in cases where different licenses have to be combined for a superior work. The determination of the license conditions on this work can be difficult, because each license has to be evaluated separately. This superior license is only valid, if it is compatible to all other licenses, which are part of the work. The permissions of this license are thus the combination of properties that are common to all licenses.

Numerous different licenses exist, which are provided by many organizations. The licenses often do not differentiate in major points or sometimes only minimally in some specific conditions. Creative Commons tries to categorize the existing licenses with the most important properties and wants to align them to the own set of licenses to achieve a form of compatibility. This increases the transparency and eases the choice of license. For this reason, the set of licenses from Creative Commons approximately covers the existing spectrum of licenses and they are a good basis for the development of methods for their machine-readable representation. In this work, the licenses of Creative Commons are thus taken exemplary for many other licenses, which are used in this application domain.

A first draft of a mapping between the REL and the Creative Commons licenses is shown in [91]. The paper explains how the intentions of the Creative Commons licenses can be expressed with the rights expressions of the MPEG-21 REL. The presented mapping allows the basic intentions of the licenses to be expressed. This draft was further developed and extended to achieve a concise solution. Although the mapping is well elaborated, the rights expressions in the REL have no legal relationship with the Creative Commons licenses. This cannot be achieved, because legal licenses can contain very specific constraints that cannot be expressed in the REL. One example is the juridical interpretation of licenses, which depends on the laws of the country where the content is consumed. It would be possible to provide separate right expressions for each country, but this would significantly increase the complexity. For this reason, the set of rights expressions was kept to a minimum. It describes the basic intentions of the license, which can be used, e.g. to notify the consumer when he presumably intends to perform an action that is not allowed in the license.

The right *adapt* expresses that a content may be adapted and published again. If the right *adapt* is granted to a consumer, he is allowed to use the content and to create a derivation of it. The right *governedAdapt* is newly defined in the OAC profile and has a similar semantic as *adapt*. Furthermore, it restricts the license on the derived content, which has to contain the same license and rights expressions as the original content. These elements foster the reuse of content, because the consumer can determine directly if he is allowed to adapt the content. The right *goverenedCopy* grants the permission to copy the content, but similar to *governedAdapt*, the license and the rights expressions have to remain the same as for the original content.

For each permission, a supplementary set of conditions can be added to further restrict the usage of the content. The element *copyrightNotice* is a notice with copyright information for the consumer. It can be added for example to show the consumer a notice before he performs the associated right. The notice can contain, for example, the license conditions. The element *nonCommercialUse* declares that the content may not be used commercially. The *sourceCode* condition can be applied for source code, which notifies the consumer that adaptations of the code have to contain the original source code or at least its accessible location within the adapted content.

The *principal* element as shown in figure 2.3 is an extension that is not

2.4. METADATA AND FILE FORMAT SPECIFICATION

required to model the intentions of the Creative Commons licenses. It was added to provide a solution for cases, where a license is applied only to a certain person or a group of people. An example is when a license free of charge is only granted to students or scientific organizations. In these cases the *principal* element can be added to specify that only the respective person or group is allowed to use this permission. A concrete person or entity can be selected with an identifier or as a holder of a specific key.

2.4.2.6 Content rendering

The rights *play, print* and *execute* are used to describe the permissions on the rendering or the presentation of the content. The author can choose, for example, to grant the corresponding right with the *copyrightNotice* to show a notice each time the consumer views the content. These rights are defined in the RDD and they can be directly used within the REL. The rights depend, however, on the type of the content, because the implementation has to support the type to be able to e.g. play or print it. This is a disadvantage, because a piece of software cannot process any content independent of its type. Nevertheless, the rights were included in the standardized OAC profile, because a design according to the REL and the RDD specification was preferred.

The REL and RDD specification also leave open how the rights are realized in a concrete implementation. The rights expressions only declare the permissions on the content. This allows an implementation either to include rendering engines for specific content types or to handle the three rights similarly. An example of such a similar realization is the extraction of the content, when one of the rights is exercised. Extraction means that the content can be saved directly in a separate file. Therefore, the consumer can open the file with an application that supports the given content type. This is a generic solution, which also works independent of the content type and is adequate for the publication of open content. For more valuable content, the implementation of rendering engines is the accurate approach.

2.4.2.7 Adaptation and aggregation

This section describes the methods for the support of adaptations and aggregations in the format. The adaptation and the aggregation of content

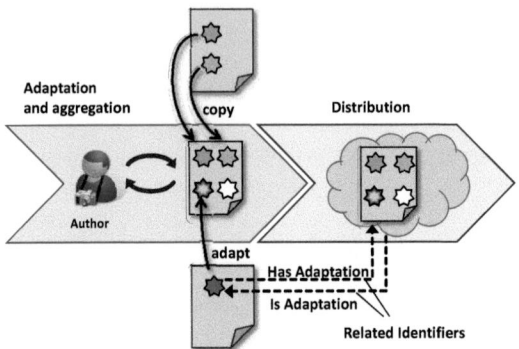

Figure 2.4: Example of adaptation and relationships

are a central aspect to ease the distribution and the reuse of content. For free distributable content, adaptations are often even desired, because the content evolves by successive modifications from different authors. In this work, the terms adapt and aggregate are used according to the corresponding definitions in the RDD. Aggregation means that an author copies and possibly combines different content into a new collection. The adaptation is defined as the copy of a content and the modification of this content. The aim is to allow an author to freely combine newly created, adapted and aggregated content into a single file, which can be published. Figure 2.4 shows an example of the adaptation and the aggregation.

The figure shows an author creating a new file which contains both aggregated and adapted content. The stars represent Items which contain the content and the metadata. The green and orange stars are aggregated, the red star was adapted. In an aggregation, a content is copied together with its metadata to the new file. To define if such a copy is allowed for the Item, the author of the original Item can use the right *governedCopy*. If the original Item provides the right *governedCopy* to the consumer, then he is allowed to perform the copy.

Similarly the rights *adapt* and *governedAdapt* express if a content may be adapted. As all these rights are machine-readable, software can use this information to notify the consumer about the permission. One example for

2.4. METADATA AND FILE FORMAT SPECIFICATION

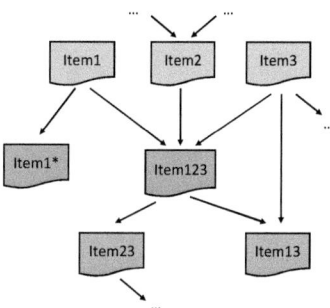

Figure 2.5: Hierarchy of relationships between derived Items

such a notification is if an author intends to release an adapted content while the original content does not allow adaptation. The software can recognize this case and can inform the consumer that the adaptation is not permitted according to the rights expressions provided with the original content.

Additionally to these rights, the related identifiers from MPEG-21 DII are used to set a link between the original and the adapted content. Every Item can have unlimited number of related identifiers. Figure 2.4 also shows these related identifiers for the adapted Item. These identifiers are set in the original and the adapted Item on the publication of the adapted Item. This relation offers advantages in the distribution of the content. A consumer who has obtained an adapted Item can find the original Item using the provided identifier. Furthermore, he can also find existing adaptations of the current Item. The relationships to the adaptations of an Item change over time, because at any time the Item can be adapted by another user. Therefore, this information is treated as *Annotation* (as specified in DID) in the metadata of the adapted Item. These relations also allow a hierarchical tree structure to be created, which shows the different stages a content went through. An example of such a structure is shown in figure 2.5. The figure shows for example that Item23 is a 2nd level derivative of the Items 1, 2 and 3.

The related identifier has the further advantage that it also specifies the attribution to the author of the original content. Some licenses require imperatively that adapted content has to declare a reference to the original content. This is also the case for the relevant Creative Commons licenses.

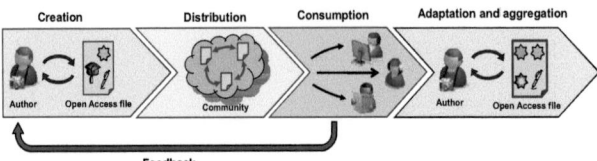

Figure 2.6: Full scenario of the file format and metadata

In these licenses, the way of referencing is, however, not precisely defined. The related identifier offers a generic and standardized method to declare this attribution within the metadata of a released file.

2.4.2.8 Feedback mechanism

In some cases, the author may be interested to get some notification about the usage of a content after he released it. He can create statistics and determine the popularity or value of his content. Distributors can also evaluate the efficiency of different methods for distribution. For this purpose, a feedback mechanism is considered that transmits notifications from the consumer back to the author. Figure 2.6 shows the enhanced scenario with the added feedback mechanism and the adaptation of content.

The mechanism is realized with MPEG-21 Event Reporting [69], which allows the metadata to declare that reports will be created and transmitted on certain events. These reports are used as notifications, which are sent back to the author. An event can be, for example, the execution of a right. In this work, two events are supported for the reports: the extraction and the derivation. The extraction event is triggered when the consumer uses one of the rights:

- *play*,
- *print*,
- *execute* or
- *governedCopy*.

These rights represent the basic usage of a content and the event is processed before the execution of the right starts. There is only one event

2.4. METADATA AND FILE FORMAT SPECIFICATION

foreseen for these four rights for simplification, as a differentiation between these rights is generally not required. If this is required in a specific application scenario, it can be supported and integrated with minimal effort. The derivation event is triggered on the execution of the rights

- *adapt* or
- *governedAdapt*.

The notification of an adaptation informs the author that the content was reused and a new Item was created from the content. This information is not only information for statistical purposes, it can also be used to create the relationship between the Items. When an author receives the report of a derived Item, he can automatically add a related identifier into the respective Item. It reduces the effort, because a manual notification is not required anymore and the automatic processing also helps to maintain the consistency between the Items.

The event reports are specified by the author, who can also decide what information is transmitted in the report. The transmitted information can be critical, because it may contain private information and should not infringe the privacy of the consumer. Furthermore, the consumer has to be aware of the information in the reports and he should confirm the transmission of reports. So it is in the interest of the author to specify reports, which are acceptable for the consumer. From the available data, the following information was considered to be of general interest to the author describing an extraction or derivation event:

- Time,
- Location,
- Identifier and
- User information.

The first three values contain the time and location of the event and the identifier of the involved Item. The user information contains the information about the user as specified in section 2.4.2.3 using the MDS standard. The report can be transmitted via http-post to a web server or via e-mail. Both methods are popular techniques of data transmission and allow an automatic processing of the transmitted information.

CHAPTER 2. METADATA FOR SHARING CONTENT

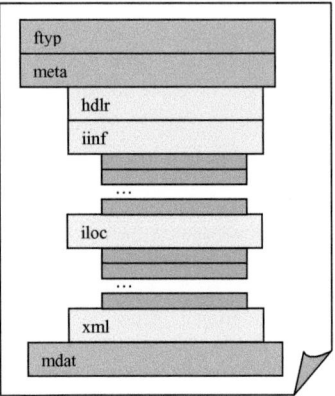

Figure 2.7: Hierarchical structure of the file format

2.4.2.9 File Format

An overview of the file format and the selected technologies was presented in section 2.4.2.1. The file format is based on the MPEG-21 File Format, because it provides an optimal integration of the MPEG-21 framework and preserves the compatibility to legacy applications. The standard is based on the ISO Base Media File Format [63], which is a generic and abstract format that is already used in many applications. It structures the file hierarchically in boxes, which comprise the resources and the metadata. The set boxes in the MPEG-21 File Format is further reduced so that only the required boxes are integrated into the system. A basic overview of the required boxes is shown in 2.7.

The boxes appear in the sequential order in an instance of the file format. The first box is the "ftyp" box, which declares the conformance to the MPEG-21 File Format and a specific value identifying the concrete system. The "meta" box comprises all the metadata of the resources. The last box with the name "mdat" contains the resources in sequential order. Within the "meta" box, the "hdlr" box defines the format of the metadata. The information about the filename and the encoding of the resource is included in the "iinf", which contains an inferior box for each resource. Similarly the

2.4. METADATA AND FILE FORMAT SPECIFICATION

"iloc" box defines the position and length of the resource in the "mdat" box with inferior boxes for each resource. The "xml" box comprises all metadata based on XML, which is attached to the resources. The root element of this metadata is specified in MPEG-21 Digital Item Declaration.

2.4.2.10 Cryptographic signatures

The MPEG-A Open Access Application Format also contains the support for cryptographic signatures, which the author can optionally use to ensure authenticity and integrity of the content. The signatures are integrated into the DID and they can be embedded for each Item as well as for the whole file. The required key infrastructure is not specified in the standard. It depends on the concrete system to provide an appropriate infrastructure for the key and the certificate management. An example for the integration of a key infrastructure is presented in section 3.4.1.1.

2.4.3 Summary and outlook

The increasing amount of free distributable content requires an elaborated and interoperable management of its common metadata to increase the exchange and the collaboration. In particular, the permanent increase of available content in the Internet demands new formats and metadata to keep content findable and manageable. The presented methods improve the efficiency in the processing and indexing of the content and its licenses. The MPEG-21 framework provides the major tools to realize this goal using a standardized file format and interoperable metadata.

The presented solutions are a first step in the license and the content management using MPEG-21 standards. Besides the licenses from Creative Commons, other licenses can also be modeled and integrated into the MPEG-21 REL. It would require more sophisticated expressions in the REL, which would also improve the precision of the machine readable licenses. Furthermore, Creative Commons is permanently enhanced to increase the compatibility and interoperability to other legal licenses. This development can be adopted into the MPEG-21 REL to advance synchronously with the permanent development. The presented solution is easily extensible to integrate these future developments in the format.

The presented methods and formats of this book were also implemented in a prototype, which is explained in section 4. The prototype realizes also additional functionalities regarding security aspects in the management and the transmission of content. This also shows the extensibility of the presented format.

This concludes the management of free distributable content with descriptive metadata. The next section broadens the scope of content and deals with more valuable content, which requires additional protection mechanism.

Chapter 3

Protection using Trusted Computing

This section investigates protection mechanisms for the management and the exchange of content. Protection mechanisms are required for content which is relevant for security like confidential documents or private information. The aim is to ensure authenticity, integrity, verifiability and confidentiality of this content. This section presents several enhancements to the protection of content using the Trusted Computing technology. Trusted Computing provides the security basis and multiple functions, which are exploited in the developed concepts. The XML standard is used as a common format for all concepts, which increases the interoperability.

The next section presents the background information, which is required to understand the developed concepts. After that, the improvement opportunities using Trusted Computing are presented and the problems in the existing solutions are described. Then, the developed concepts are explained in detail.

3.1 Fundamentals

The protection mechanisms are differentiated in three categories: encryption, signature and authentication. The following sections introduce standards and technologies for these three categories. The standards and

50   CHAPTER 3. PROTECTION USING TRUSTED COMPUTING

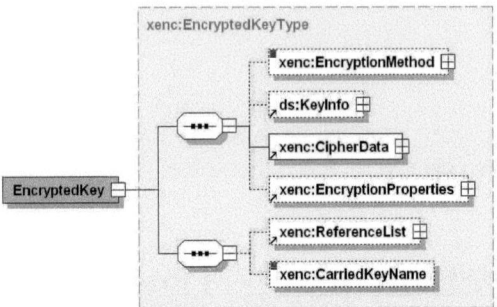

Figure 3.1: Syntax of the *EncryptedKey* element

technologies are briefly described to understand their main functionalities, which are relevant for the developed concepts.

3.1.1 Encrypted data in XML

One method to ensure the confidentiality of data is the application of encryption algorithms. To exchange encrypted data, XML can be used as transportation format. This can be achieved with the XML Encryption Syntax and Processing (XMLEnc) standard [56]. This standard defines a syntax for the transportation of encrypted data together with information about the algorithm, the parameters or the keys. This information is used in the recipient for the decryption of the ciphertext. Furthermore, it allows to specify the process of the encryption and decryption. The XML standard is not limited to the transportation of encrypted XML documents, it allows to embed any type of encrypted data in a XML format.

One functionality of the XMLEnc standard is the syntax of the *EncryptedKey* element. It is shown in figure 3.1, which was created with the software Altova XMLSpy [35].

The element is used to transport an encrypted key to a recipient. The recipient has the related secret to decrypt the key. The element *EncryptedKey* has an optional attribute with the name *Recipient*. It contains an application-specific string, which specifies the recipient of the encrypted key.

3.1. FUNDAMENTALS

The encryption algorithm is declared in the *EncryptionMethod* element. The *KeyInfo* element originates from the XMLDSig standard and is used to specify the key which was used for the encryption. Within the *KeyInfo* element, the key can be declared in different ways. Examples are a reference with a name or a X.509 certificate. The element *CipherData* contains the encrypted key to be transported. The encrypted key can be either embedded within the element or associated with a reference. The *EncryptionProperties* element specifies additional information about the encryption, for example the date of the encryption. The element *ReferenceList* declares one or more links to other elements which contain data that was encrypted by the transported key. The other elements can be other *EncryptedKey* or *EncryptedData* elements. The *CarriedKeyName* element associates an identifier or name to the transported key.

3.1.2 MPEG-21 IPMP

The MPEG-21 standards were developed to design and to enable the interoperable exchange and the use of content between different systems. The content is not limited to free distributable content, but also for example confidential content with a high value. The MPEG-21 standards include methods to ensure authenticity, integrity and confidentiality of exchanged content.

One standard in the MPEG-21 framework was developed to provide such protection mechanisms to the content. This standard is the Intellectual Property Management and Protection Components (IPMP) [73], which has the identifier ISO/IEC 21000-4. It defines a simple mechanism to embed protection information within the DID. This protection information contains an alternative way of representing the elements from the DID with added protection information. The protection information is specified in the IPMP Info Descriptor, which defines the parameters and the tools to realize the protection. Furthermore, the standard contains an IPMP General Info Descriptor, which can be used to declare general information about an Item as a whole. The IPMP standard enables the control of the content with generic containers that can transport the required information. The standard does not specify particular cryptographic algorithms, keys, devices, certificates or other components for the protection. For the realization of an IPMP solu-

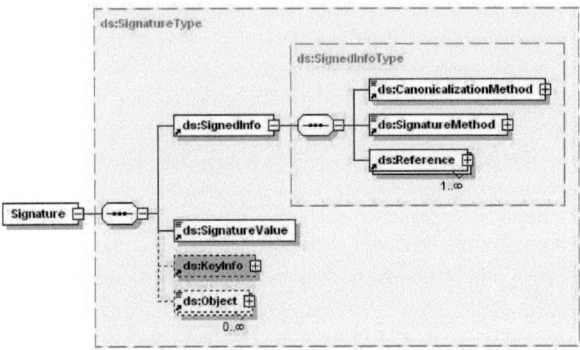

Figure 3.2: Structure of a XML signature

tion, a concise protection concept has to be developed and integrated into the standard.

3.1.3 Digital signatures in XML

The MPEG-21 standards allow the integration of Digital Signatures according to the XML Signature Syntax and Processing (XMLDSig) standard [50]. This standard specifies a generic framework to represent a signature in the XML format. A signature conform to XMLDSig can be declared in three forms: detached, enveloped or enveloping. A detached signature is separated from the signed XML document and only refers to the document via a URL. If the signature is integrated in a document and it signs parts of this document, the signature is an enveloped signature. An enveloping signature contains the signed XML document directly within the signature document.

The basic structure of a XML-signature is shown in figure 3.2. The figure was created using the software Altova XMLSpy [35].

The root element is the *Signature* element, which contains all values of the signature. The first element in the *Signature* element is the *SignedInfo* element, which comprises properties of the signature. One of these properties

3.1. FUNDAMENTALS

is the method for canonicalization, which is described by the *CanonicalizationMethod* element. The canonicalization for example removes semantically irrelevant characters (e.g. spaces, line breaks) of the document to create a homogeneous document for the signature. The *SignatureMethod* element declares the used algorithms for the signature and the *Reference* element contains references as URIs to the documents which are signed. The *SignatureValue* element contains the resulting value of the signature operation. The certificates and the public key, which corresponds to the private key of the signature, are in the *KeyInfo* element. They can be used for the verification of the signature. The element *Object* is an optional element, which can be used to include additional data in the signature.

One example of such additional data is a timestamp, which is explained in the following section.

3.1.3.1 Qualified timestamp

A qualified timestamp uses cryptographic algorithms to bind a specific date and time to a document. The aim is to prove that the document existed at a certain point in time. Such a timestamp is created by a Timestamping Authority (TSA), which is a trusted third party with a precise clock. A client can request a timestamp from a TSA using specific protocols. The most common used protocol is the IETF standard Time-Stamp Protocol (TSP) [37], which describes the messages between the TSA and the client. This standard is also used in the developed concept in this book. Other standards for this functionality are the ISO Standard ISO/IEC 18014 [65, 66, 67] and the ANSI ASC X9.95 Standard [38], which are not explained further in this book, because they only differentiate in some application scenarios. They provide the same basic functionalities as the TSP standard and within the scope of this book, they can replace transparently the TSP standard if required. The following section explains the TSP standard more in detail.

Creation of timestamps The TSP standard enables the creation of a signed timestamp for a given document. Figure 3.3 shows the process of the creation of a timestamp and the exchanged data between the client and the TSA.

54 CHAPTER 3. PROTECTION USING TRUSTED COMPUTING

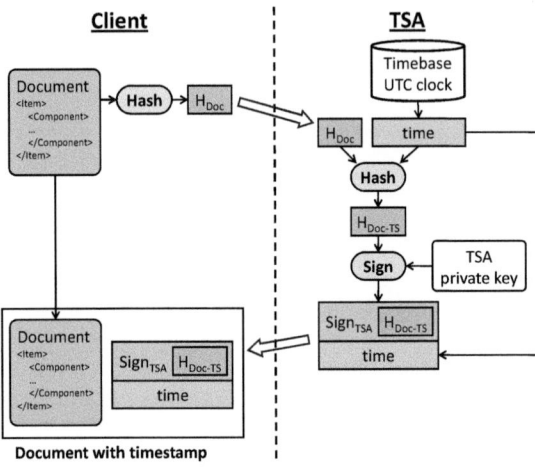

Figure 3.3: Creation of a qualified timestamp according to the Time-Stamp Protocol

The exchanged data additionally contains a nonce to prevent replay attacks. The nonce is not depicted in the figure for simplicity reasons. In the first step, the hash value of the document is calculated and transferred to the TSA. The hash value is sufficient, because it is directly connected to the document. As the TSA receives only the hash value, the confidentiality of the document itself is not at risk. In the next step, the TSA combines the current time with the hash value and calculates the overall hash value of the combination. The resulting value is then signed using the private key of the TSA. The created signature, the hash value of the document and the time value are then transferred to the client. These values compose the qualified timestamp of the document, which can be validated by any party.

Validation The validation of a qualified timestamp proves that the respective document was existent at a specific point in time. To perform the validation, the verifier requires the document and the signature with the time value which was created by the TSA. The verifier starts with the same procedure, which was performed for the creation. The verifier calculates the hash

3.1. FUNDAMENTALS

value of the document and attaches the given time value to the hash value. The combination of both values is hashed again and the resulting hash value is used as reference value for the comparison with the received signature. Then, the verifier has to obtain the public key of the TSA. Depending on the relationship to the respective TSA, this can be secured with certificates to verify the trustworthiness of the TSA. The public key is applied to the signature and the result is compared to the previously calculated reference value. If both values are equal, the signature is valid and the document was existent at the given time value.

3.1.3.2 XML Advanced Electronic Signatures

The XML Advanced Electronic Signatures (XAdES) [51] is an extension of the XMLDSig standard that allows to apply more sophisticated signatures with further enhancements. The latest versions of the standard were published by ETSI [12].

XAdES defines additional profiles for use cases that require additional security features. Examples of such use cases are the validation of the point in time of the signing operation or the long-term archiving of signatures. These examples show that qualified timestamps are required in the XAdES standard to support such an use case. Thus, the XAdES supports the representation of timestamps in XML and specifies a syntax and a semantic for the respective elements. These elements are structured with an abstract and generic type, the *GenericTimeStampType*, which is a common basis for all supported use cases. For each use case the *GenericTimeStampType* is derived and extended to support all requirements of the use case. Figure 3.4 was created with the software Altova XMLSpy [35] and depicts the structure of the *GenericTimeStampType*.

The *Include* and *ReferenceInfo* elements specify the document which is signed with the timestamp. *Include* specifies a reference to the document, while the *ReferenceInfo* contains directly the hash value of the document. The *CanonicalizationMethod* is a common structure required for the creation of signatures in XML. The *EncapsulatedTimeStamp* contains the timestamp in an encapsulated form as specified in the Time-Stamp Protocol standard [37]. The *XMLTimeStamp* element provides a representation of the timestamp in XML. This is a placeholder, as the structure of the *XML-*

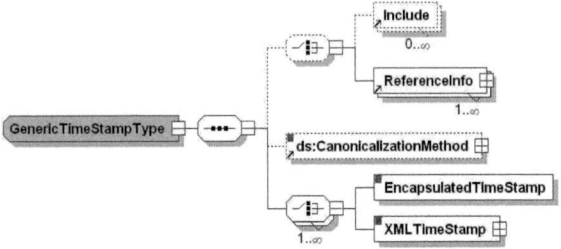

Figure 3.4: Structure of the GenericTimeStampType

TimeStamp is not yet standardized.

Two types derive from the *GenericTimeStampType*: the *XAdESTimeStampType* and the *OtherTimeStampType*. The types differentiate in their method of referencing the data which is timestamped. For each use case a derivative is created from this common type, which provides the required fields.

This concludes the standards for the creation of qualified timestamps and its representation in XML. The next section introduces the Trusted Computing technology, which is used as security basis for the developed concepts.

3.1.4 Trusted Computing

Trusted Computing is a trust concept which ensures that a system behaves in a specific manner for a certain purpose. The Trusted Computing technology is specified by the Trusted Computing Group (TCG) [29] with the ambition to enhance the security in computers and devices. The TCG is a consortia of international industrial partners, which developed open standards for Trusted Computing platforms. These platforms provide a higher level of security on the basis of a hardware security module, the Trusted Platform Module (TPM) [103, 104, 105]. The specification of the TPM was adopted by ISO/IEC and standardized in [59, 60, 61, 62].

The TPM is basically a secure cryptoprocessor with tamper protection, which is designed for the wide integration in many platforms and devices. The TPM does not fulfill the requirements for high-security, as its capabilities are

3.1. FUNDAMENTALS

usually limited regarding key length and performance. But as a hardware security module it provides basic cryptographic functions to enhance the security of a platform. The TPM is widely distributed in many devices and platforms, which qualifies it as a good basis for the application in extensive environments, for example in corporations.

3.1.4.1 Trusted Platform Module (TPM)

The TPM is a hardware security module, which is integrated into the platform. It provides the basis for the security of several cryptographic operations. The TPM is a passive element which other system components have to address to perform specific operations. Example of these system components are a Trusted Computing aware operating systems or applications. The TPM serves for two main purposes: secure storage and integrity measurements. Furthermore, it stores and creates several special keys and certificates. These purposes and the special keys are explained in the following sections.

3.1.4.2 Secure storage

The TPM can create and securely store critical data like cryptographic keys or certificates. Symmetric keys can only be generated and stored, but not used for encryption operations, as the TPM specification does not require a processing unit for a symmetric algorithm. Asymmetric keys can be used for the encryption and the signing of data. Every TPM supports the RSA algorithm with key sizes of 512, 1024, and 2048 bits. The TPM has also a key generation engine, which can be used to generate asymmetric keys. The generated keys can be either returned to the requesting application or they can be stored in the TPM.

For the storage of the key, the TPM supports two different types: migratable or non-migratable keys. A migratable key can be transferred to another TPM in a restrictive protocol to ensure the uniqueness of the key. A non-migratable key is not allowed to be transferred and always stays within the specific TPM, which created the key.

Migratable and non-migratable keys, are protected by the TPM that the private part of the key never leaves the TPM unencrypted. If a key has to be exported out of the TPM, it is encrypted before it is exported. This is for example required if the memory of the TPM is exhausted. The usage of a private key stored in the TPM for signing or encryption operation is only performed within the TPM. This ensures also the correct execution of the operation. The TPM can also prove to external parties that the key was generated and stored in the TPM. For this prove, an AIK key is used, which is explained in section 3.1.4.5.

3.1.4.3 Integrity measurements

The TPM has a set of registers, the Platform Configuration Registers (PCR), which are used for the verification of the integrity of the platform. During the boot procedure of the platform, the PCRs are involved to create hash values of the executed software components. When the boot procedure is finished, the PCRs contain characteristic values of the running software components, which represent the system state. The values can be used to determine if the current state of the platform can be trusted, i.e. if it works as expected.

The PCR values can be also transmitted to another client or a trusted third party, which performs the verification of the system state. This method is called Remote Attestation.

The functions for the integrity measurement are not used in this book and are not explained more in detail. The developed concepts are compatible with these measurements and can be integrated in an operating system which applies the integrity measurements to protect the operating system.

3.1.4.4 Internal keys and certificates

A TPM contains a set of internal keys and certificates, which are used to prove authenticity and integrity of the TPM towards external parties. The Endorsement Credential is a certificate issued by the manufacturer, which certifies the Endorsement Key (EK). The EK is a 2048 bit key pair, which can be used for signing operations. The EK is not migratable and it should not be used directly for any signing operation because the key allows the identification of the TPM. Furthermore, the TPM contains the certificates

3.1. FUNDAMENTALS

Conformance Credential, Platform Credential and Validation Credential to prove the correct manufacturing and integration in the platform.

Furthermore, the TPM contains the Storage Root Key (SRK), which is used as the principal key for storing generated or external keys. The SRK is a non-migratable 2048 bit RSA key pair and it is created when the ownership of the TPM is taken. The taking of the ownership corresponds to the initialization of the TPM, which generates a SRK and sets a password for it. For any further usage of the SRK, the user has to provide the password again for authentication. The SRK is the root of a key hierarchy structured as a tree. The SRK encrypts one or more other keys, also called Storage Keys (SK), which are the inferior keys of the SRK. A SK can be used to encrypt other keys or data. The encrypted Storage Keys and the data in the hierarchy can be also stored outside of the TPM on an unprotected storage. This is not problematic, because the exported key or data is encrypted with the superior SK before the export. Thus, an exported key or data can be only decrypted within the TPM.

3.1.4.5 Attestation Identity Keys and PrivacyCA

The EK is the certified key of the TPM, but it cannot be used directly, because it would reveal the identity of the TPM and thus prevent anonymity. The Attestation Identity Keys (AIK) allow the verification of the platform or internal values towards an external party while preserving the anonymity of the platform. An example of such an internal value is a private key, which was generated and stored within the TPM. The public part of this key can be signed with an AIK within the TPM to certify the origin of the key. An external party can verify this signature to ensure that the private part related to the public key is protected by the TPM.

An AIK can only be used to sign internal data. A TPM can create multiple AIKs, which are derived from the EK and replace the EK in the verification procedure. An AIK is a 2048 bit RSA key and is not migratable. To verify the authenticity of an AIK, an AIK credential is required, which is issued by the PrivacyCA. The PrivacyCA is a trusted third party, which can verify the conformance of a TPM using the provided certificates. The PrivacyCA issues and validates certificates for the EK or an AIK. The PrivacyCA ensures that a valid certificate on the EK or an AIK originates of an authentic TPM. A user may trust the PrivacyCA directly or a superior certification authority if a hierarchical Public Key Infrastructure (PKI) is realized.

Alternatively, the Direct Anonymous Attestation (DAA) [42] allows the verification of an AIK without a trusted third party. It uses a zero knowledge protocol to prove the authenticity of the AIK directly to the other party. This protocol is available since the version 1.2 of the TPM specification.

3.1.4.6 Timestamping

The Trusted Computing technology can be used to create qualified timestamps. The TPM contains a counter, which can count short intervals in time, which are called ticks. This tick counter does not provide the time as an absolute universal time clock. The tick counter provides a relative value, which is the number of ticks passed from the moment the timing session is started. To get an absolute time base, the tick counter has to be linked with an external universal time clock. The TCG specifies a protocol to create this link in [103]. This leads to a significant different composition of a timestamp from the TPM in comparison with a traditional timestamp. The timestamp created by the TPM is called TPM-timestamp in the following sections. The mentioned protocol and the tick counter are explained in the next sections.

3.1.4.7 Tick counter

The tick counter is an internal TPM functionality, which counts the passed time in ticks beginning from the start of the timing session. The figure 3.5 shows the functionality of the tick counter.

At a certain point in time, in the figure t_1, the tick timing session is initialized and the counter starts to count the ticks. The specification leaves it up to the manufacturer to define, when the initialization is performed. The need to initialize the counter depends on the power supply of the whole platform. As there are different conditions for example in a PC desktop or a mobile device, the manufacturer has to decide about the maintenance of the counter.

When the user wants to retrieve the current counter value, the command "getTicks" can be sent to the TPM. This is the time t_2 in the figure. The

3.1. FUNDAMENTALS

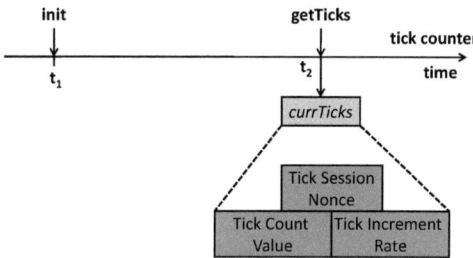

Figure 3.5: Tick counter and its output

result is the currTicks value, which is an aggregation of the three values: Tick Session Nonce, Tick Count Value and Tick Increment Rate. The Tick Count Value is the current number of ticks of the counter and the Tick Increment Rate specifies the rate at which the ticks are counted. The relationship between Tick Increment Rate and seconds is a parameter defined by the manufacturer, because it is up to the manufacturer to define a timing source for the counter. According to the specification, the timing ticks should be a reliable and tamper-proof source to achieve the required security, e.g. an internal clock circuit within the TPM.

The Tick Session Nonce is a nonce, which identifiers the current timing session. The initialization of this nonce is not imperatively defined in the specification. To achieve a secure operation, the tick counter must be set to zero and a new nonce must be generated for each initialization of a timing session. This allows to assign a Tick Counter Value to a timing session. It allows to verify that a Tick Counter Value belongs to the current session. It enables the detection of a re-initialization of the counter between consecutive executions of the getTicks command.

3.1.4.8 Tickstamp

The tick counter provides the reliable counting of the time. The TPM allows to create a signature on the tick counter using an AIK key. The result is the tickstamp, which has a similar structure as a traditional timestamp. The figure 3.6 shows the process for the creation of a tickstamp and its structure.

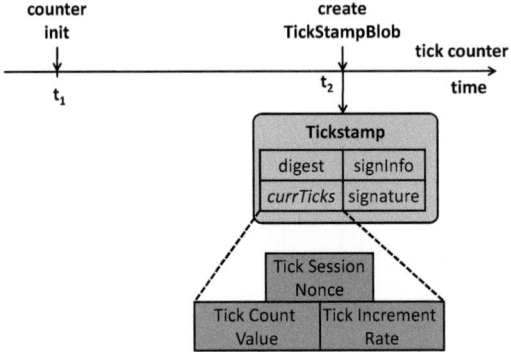

Figure 3.6: Creation of a tickstamp

Similar as for the tick counter, the command "TickStampBlob" may be executed at a certain time t_2 to create the tickstamp. As input for this command, the TPM requires among others the reference to the key for the signature and the digest (hash value) of the document to sign.

The answer of the command is the tickstamp, which consists of four values: digest, currTicks, signInfo and signature. The digest is the hash value of the document and the currTicks is the current value of the tick counter as shown in section 3.1.4.7. The signInfo contains data in a structure as specified in [104], which was created during the signing. The signature is the value of the signature over all data in this structure. The key used for the signature is an AIK, which proves that the signature was performed by a TPM within a trusted platform. This allows to prove the recipient that the tickstamp was created in a secure environment.

The tickstamp thus links the digest to the current Tick Count Value. In the next step, the Tick Count Value is linked to an universal time clock to obtain an absolute TPM-timestamp.

3.1.4.9 Timestamp Protocol

The TCG specifies a protocol to create a timestamp within the TPM, which is verifiable by external parties. This TPM-timestamp consists of two

3.1. FUNDAMENTALS

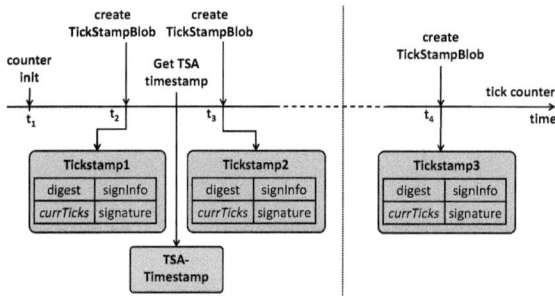

Figure 3.7: Timestamp protocol sequence

steps: the first step is to link a tick counter to an universal time clock and the second step is the effective signature over the document together with the current time. The whole process is shown in figure 3.7.

Anytime after the initialization of the timing session, the protocol can start with the first step, in which the tick counter is linked to the universal time. A tickstamp, Tickstamp1, is created with a digest on the text "Tick Stamp". This text is defined in the specifications. This links the Tick Count Value and the session nonce with the signature.

Then a traditional timestamp from a TSA is obtained according to the protocol presented in section 3.1.3.1. The hash of the data in Tickstamp1 is sent to the TSA, which integrates an absolute timestamp from an universal time clock and signs it.

After the reception of the TSA-timestamp, a second tickstamp, Tickstamp2, is created using a digest of TSA-timestamp. The second tickstamp is required to have an upper limit of the amount of time passed between Tickstamp1 and the TSA-timestamp. The tick counter thus has an uncertainty, which is limited by Tickstamp1 and Tickstamp2. To an external party, it can be only proven that the universal time is between the two Tick Count Values of both tickstamps, but the exact Tick Count Value cannot be determined. Tickstamp1 and Tickstamp2 are the lower and upper boundaries of the current time and the interval between both tickstamps should be kept to a minimum. Otherwise, an external party can decide to reject the created

64   CHAPTER 3. PROTECTION USING TRUSTED COMPUTING

timestamp, because the uncertainty of the timestamp is too high.

After the creation of this link, the respective timing session is set up for the creation of TPM-timestamps. As long as the timing session is valid, the TPM can create an unlimited amount of timestamps without any further data exchange with external parties. The timing session terminates if the tick counter is re-initialized, for example in the case of a power loss. To create a TPM-timestamp, the hash value is calculated over the document and with this a tickstamp, Tickstamp3, is created. This completes the link between the time reference value coming from the TSA and the Tick Count Value of the last tickstamp. With all these values, the point in time when the document was timestamped can be determined. All three tickstamps and the TSA-timestamp together with the AIK credentials form the timestamp created by the TPM. The values can be transmitted with the document to a recipient, which can then verify the tickstamps and the TSA-timestamp to determine the correctness of the created TPM-timestamp.

3.1.4.10 TCG Software Stack

To integrate the TPM into the operating system, a device driver is required, which adds the TPM as a device. Then, applications or the operating system can access the TPM and its functions using a low-level API. This API, however, should not be accessed directly by applications, because it does not support concurrent access.

For this reason, the TCG Software Stack (TSS) [102] is on top of the device driver as intermediate software layer between the driver and the application or operating system. The TSS runs in the user mode of the operating system as a service or daemon. It provides an interface, the TSS Service Provider Interface (TSPI), to the other applications, which allows them to access comfortably the functions of the TPM. The TSS implements a conversion of parameters from the TSPI to the low-level API functions of the TPM to reduce the efforts for a low-level implementation in the applications. The TSS also multiplexes the access to the TPM, therefore, multiple applications can access the TPM functions simultaneously. A separate context is created for each application and the conflicts in the simultaneous access of a function is resolved.

The TSS manages also the storage of keys, which are protected by the

3.1. FUNDAMENTALS

TPM. These keys are encrypted with the SRK or an inferior SK using the mentioned key hierarchy. The TSS provides two types of storage for these keys: the User Persistent Storage or the System Persistent Storage. The User Persistent Storage stores keys, which belong to a specific user. The System Persistent Storage contains keys, which are available for all users of the system.

3.1.5 Web based authentication with OpenID

This section presents the authentication of users with the web-based Single Sign On system OpenID. To understand the concepts and architecture of the OpenID system, a short introduction of Single Sign On (SSO) is presented. Then, the architecture and functionalities of the OpenID system are explained in detail.

3.1.5.1 Web-based Single Sign On

A Single Sign On (SSO) system provides an authentication mechanism, which allows to validate the user identity for multiple services. These services are provided by third parties, which request the identification and authentication of a user. The advantage for the user is a single authentication for multiple services of the participating third parties at once. Web based SSO-systems are a web service, which perform the authentication of the user for multiple websites. After the authentication, the user is automatically logged in for the websites in liaison with the SSO-system. The advantage for the user is that he only has to authenticate himself once towards the SSO-system and after that, he has access to all websites. Another advantage is that the authentication secrets are only shared and exchanged with the SSO-system. Other websites do not receive any authentication data, because they only exchange the information confidentially with the SSO-system. The next section presents the OpenID system, which is a SSO-system providing the mentioned functionalities.

3.1.5.2 OpenID

The OpenID system was developed to establish SSO services in the Internet. The system is specified in [52] and presented in [89]. By the end of 2009, over 1 billion OpenID enabled accounts were created and several providers worldwide integrated the support of OpenID [23].

The OpenID specification defines the protocol between three parties: the User Agent, the Relaying Party and the OpenID Provider. The User Agent is the browser on the client machine, which is operated by the user. The user wants to authenticate himself towards a website, which is called the Relaying Party in OpenID. During an authentication, the Relaying Party is redirecting the user to the OpenID Provider, which shares the secrets with the user. If the authentication with the Provider was successful, the user is redirected back to the Relaying Party and is logged in at the site. The specification defines the format of the exchanged messages and their methods of protection.

OpenID specification does not require a single central authentication instance, because everyone can set up an OpenID Provider with proper user accounts. This enhances the privacy and the independence of other parties. Furthermore, an OpenID Provider can also store personal user information, like the e-mail address. The user can control, whether this information may be transmitted to the Relaying Party or not. As OpenID is a web-based protocol, it is independent of the operating system. The User Agent only requires a browser, which is available for all common operating systems. The Relaying Party is a web service which uses an additional library to support the OpenID protocol for the user authentication.

Identifier The identifier of the user is a central aspect in the OpenID specifications. An identifier in OpenID is a Uniform Resource Identifier (URI) [39] or an Extensible Resource Identifier (XRI) [90]. An URI is a string of characters with a given syntax, which enables the identification of abstract or physical resources. XRI is based on URI, but provides more sophisticated methods for the structuring and delegation of identifiers.

Each user has an identifier, which is unique within a Provider. This identifier can be understood as a username. A part of the user identifier is a reference to the Provider. Every identifier allows the discovery of the Provider using the XRI resolution protocol [106]. The XRI standard is based on the Domain Name System (DNS) Resolution system and also specifies the exchanged information, which allows the negotiation of the Provider capabilities. The detailed protocol is not relevant and is thus not explained further

3.1. FUNDAMENTALS

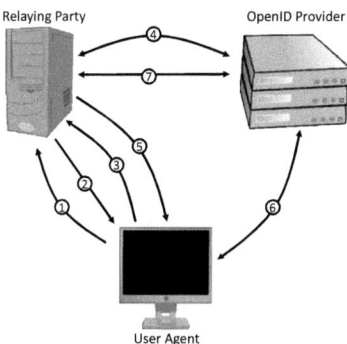

Figure 3.8: OpenID redirect protocol

in this book. The application of the discovery within the OpenID protocol is shown in the next section.

Authentication protocol The OpenID protocol consists of several steps to exchange data between the User Agent, the Relaying Party and the Provider. The figure 3.8 shows these three parties and the steps of the protocol.

The user wants to authenticate himself to the Relying Party in order to access user-specific services. In step one, the user requests the page of the Relaying Party, which provides a form for the authentication. The User Agent receives the page in step two and asks the user to enter his OpenID identifier in the form. In step three, the User Agent sends the filled form back to the Relaying Party.

Then, the Relaying Party performs the XRI resolution on the identifier to determine the Provider. The Relaying Party establishes a connection with the Provider in step four and references it with an associate handle. Optionally the Relaying Party can secure the connection with a shared secret, which is negotiated between the two parties.

In step five, the Relaying Party redirects the User Agent to the Provider. After that, the Provider exchanges information with the User Agent for the authentication in step six. The authentication method is not specified in OpenID and it is up to the Provider to define a mechanism, which allows the re-identification of a registered user. A method often used is a password authentication via web forms.

When the authentication is finished, the Provider redirects the User Agent back to the Relaying Party. The result of the authentication is transmitted within the redirect, which informs the Relaying Party if the authentication was successful.

In the last step, the Relaying Party verifies if the authentication result originates from the Provider. For this validation, the Relaying Party can use the shared secret, which was negotiated before with the Provider. The Relaying Party may connect to the Provider, if it requires more data for the validation. If the authentication result is valid, the user is authenticated in the Relaying Party and typically the OpenID identifier is associated to the connection with the User Agent.

Security mechanisms The OpenID specification applies several security enhancements to protect the authentication process. The previous section already mentioned the shared secret between the Relaying Party and the Provider, which is obtained using a Diffie-Hellman key exchange. This preserves the integrity and the authenticity of the exchanged information to verify the authentication result.

Furthermore, OpenID requires a nonce within the redirect from the Provider back to the Relaying Party to prevent replay attacks. The specification also recommends to use Transport Layer Security (TLS) [49] between the User Agent and the Provider to have a basic protection against man-in-the-middle attacks and eavesdropping.

The user is authenticated in a single instance, the Provider, which also simplifies the password management of the user. Many websites implement an own password authentication, which requires the user to remember a password for each site. The usage of the same password on multiple sites increases the security, because only the interception of the password on one of the sites grants the attacker permission to all sites. The OpenID system reduces the possible targets for an attack to one site, the Provider, which can apply sophisticated security methods to ensure the confidentiality of the authentication secrets. The central login also helps the user in the recognition of the authentication page of the Provider. This helps to prevent phishing attacks, in which the attacker tries to bring the user to perform an erroneous login to a fraudulent site. This method allows an attacker to obtain the password of a user.

3.2 Problem statement

The aim is to enhance the protection of exchanged content in XML based content management systems. To achieve this aim, authenticity, integrity, verifiability and confidentiality of the content has to be ensured. Authenticity, integrity and verifiability can be provided by signatures, confidentiality is realized with the encryption of the content. The Trusted Computing technology with the TPM enables the enhancement of the security in several aspects, because it provides the basis for the execution of cryptographic algorithms and the storage of security critical data like for example secret keys. Furthermore, the TPM implements additional functionalities, which can be exploited to enhance the security.

The provided security should be oriented to the user, who can self-determined rule over all his data. The aim is to achieve complete transparency for the user, even when strict confidentiality is provided towards third parties. It is up to the user to decide, which data may be passed to which user. This is the basic principle for successful content management systems.

The integration of signatures and encryption ensures the most important security requirements. Both security mechanisms require for their realization a key management concept and a user authentication mechanism. The TPM provides functionalities for the creation and storage of keys on a platform, but there is no overall concept for the key and the user management on distributed platforms. This superior architecture has to be developed, which combines the TPM technology with the MPEG-21 standards to realize a concise and comprehensive system. One principal task is to combine the standards in such a way that the conformance of each standard is not infringed. The semantic and structure should remain intact and only be enriched with additional fields whenever possible. If this enhancement is infeasible, the required modifications should be minimized.

In this work, the three concepts are presented: a concept for secure content transmission, timestamps in digital signatures and user authentication. These concepts are explained in the following sections.

3.2.1 Secure content storage and transmission

To protect confidential content from a fraudulent access, encryption mechanisms have to be applied to ensure that only the correct user can view the content. On a system with many users, an encrypted storage is required. This storage can be performed in the operating system or in the application. In the operating system, an appropriate modification or configuration is required to enable the encryption. For example additional drivers for the encryption of devices have to be loaded. An encryption on the application level is independent of system modifications and only requires an interoperable format for all applications. It also has to be defined how the description of the encryption is integrated to preserve the compatibility and the interoperability.

Besides the secure storage, the content also should be transmitted between users on different platforms. The content can be transmitted securely in encrypted form to another party, but the exchange of the encryption key of the content is still required. If the key is also encrypted and embedded into the file with the content, it would enable the confidential and the secure exchange of the content. Furthermore, it allows the transmission of the encrypted content with any method and protocol. This method does not require any changes in the system or in the method of transmission. The security is implemented in the application, which requires a conform implementation to support the format.

In this scenario, two methods have to be developed: the encryption of the content and the secure exchange of the encryption keys. The encryption of the content can be realized with an extension of the metadata in the file format to support and describe the encryption. The MPEG-21 IPMP standard can be applied to describe tools for the encryption and its parameters. The MPEG-21 standard has no direct support for Trusted Computing, therefore, the standards need to be aligned and combined. The required parts of the

3.2. PROBLEM STATEMENT

IPMP standard have to be selected and are integrated into the metadata of the content.

Besides the encryption of the content, the respective key has to be transferred confidentially to the recipient. An appropriate method for the key management has to be found, which uses the Trusted Computing technology to protect the keys. The keys must be encrypted and integrated into the metadata. A method for the integration has to be used, which is conform to the MPEG-21 standards and which does not influence the distribution of the content. The distribution can include the copy and aggregation of Items in multiple files.

An Item can incorporate a signature to ensure the authenticity, the integrity and the verifiability of the content. It enables the verification of the author of a content and proves that the content has not been modified during the distribution. As already mentioned in section 2.4.2.10, a signature can be embedded within each Item or for the whole file. A concept for the embedding of the signatures must be developed together with a method for its creation. The signature must remain intact during the distribution of the content. The distribution also includes an autonomous copy or aggregation of the content by intermediate parties, which may not affect the validity of the signature.

The overall aim is to achieve a decentralized system that no central third party is required for the key management. The content keys must remain in the control of the user and allow him to decide how and to whom the content may be transferred.

3.2.2 Timestamps in digital signatures

In this concept digital signatures are extended by the integration of TPM-timestamps. The TPM-timestamp is issued and signed by the TPM and a trusted third party, which allows an external party to verify the timestamp. Such a timestamp within the signature proves that the document was existent in that specific point in time.

To include a traditional timestamp in a signature, a connection to a trusted third party, the TSA, is required to obtain the signed timestamp. This connection can be cumbersome in some scenarios, for example for mobile devices. The Trusted Computing technology can be used to enable the creation of signatures with qualified timestamps in offline environments. The specified protocol from the TCG allows to create a timestamp with a TPM, which can be verified by external parties. The protocol, however, does not describe methods for the integration of the created values in a signature. These values are binary data, which need to be mapped to existing XML elements with the appropriate semantic. The elements come from existing standards, which may already support parts of the required elements. The corresponding elements have to be determined and if no appropriate element can be found, a new representation of the values has to be defined and specified. XML signatures are widely used for the signing of XML documents, also for example in several MPEG-21 standards.

Furthermore, the new timestamp with the extended values has to be integrated into the XMLDSig or XAdES signature standards. Both standards are examined and a possible way of integration is presented. While XAdES contains methods for the representation of qualified timestamps, the XMLDSig standard does not support this functionality. The ideal aim is a solution which is compatible and integrable with both standards. The representation of the values also has to be optimized regarding the required modifications of the standards. The extension of the standard has to be elaborated accurately that existing implementations of the standard remain compatible. Also the added extensions should be minimized, to keep the changes for the support of the feature to a minimum.

3.2.3 User authentication

User authentication identifies the user of the platform, which enables to determine if the user is allowed to access a content. To realize user authentication, management facilities are required, for example for the creation or deletion of users. This user management is an important aspect, because the access to security-critical content may be only granted to a specific user or group of users. The content creator has to be able to choose the respective users from a list. The list can be provided by a centralized service, where all users are registered. Furthermore, the service should be web-based, open and standardized to support the integration of the service in other systems. In this book, the OpenID system is used as it provides a standardized and interoperable method for a web-based user management.

3.3. COMPARISON WITH OTHER SYSTEMS

The OpenID standard does not specify the method of how the authentication of the user has to be performed. The common approach in the existing OpenID-systems in the Internet is the authentication with a user name and a password. The password is the secret of the user, which differentiates him from other persons. The user can authenticate to a OpenID Provider by providing the password that belongs to his username. The OpenID Provider compares the given password with a stored value from the registration of the user. If the values match, the user is authenticated. This method is convenient, but it is also the source of several security issues.

One of these security limitations in OpenID is the phishing attack, which is presented in [54]. In this attack, the web page of the OpenID Provider is imitated on another server. Then, the attacker tries to bring the user to input his password on the rogue web page. If the user does so, the user reveals his password to the attacker, who can then authenticate himself to the real OpenID Provider as the user. The attacker may then redirect the user to the desired relying party, therefore, the performed attack is not noticeable anymore to the user. The revelation of the password is also not recognizable by the user in upcoming authentications or another usage of the system.

In this book, the TPM is used to prevent phishing attacks and to replace the user name and password authentication with a more secure protocol. The messages of the protocol have to be defined and the TPM is used for the key storage. The User Agent is extended with additional functionalities to support the protocol. The User Agent is also able to connect to the TPM and to use its functions for the execution of the protocol. The user authentication is performed locally to the TPM. If the user can authenticate towards the TPM, the User Agent can perform the protocol with the OpenID Provider. The details of this method have to be elaborated and specified.

3.3 Comparison with other systems

This section compares the mentioned problem statements with existing solutions and concepts. The existing solutions are presented and compared to the goals in this book.

3.3.1 Concepts for secure content exchange

There exists a large number of applications, which enable the protected storage and exchange of content. The scope in this book is the usage of the MPEG-21 technology in combination with Trusted Computing to realize a secure and interoperable solution. Currently, there is only one system to the best knowledge of the author, which uses Trusted Computing as protection mechanism in MPEG-21. This system is SmartRM, which is explained in the following section.

3.3.1.1 SmartRM system

The goal of the SmartRM system [26] is to ease the exchange of content while protecting the confidentiality of content. A user who is the author of a content, can package it into a special file, which is then shared with other users. The files are encrypted and can be exchanged arbitrarily with any method or protocol. The decryption is separately granted for each access, therefore, the author can decide at any time, who can access the content. This is enabled with a centralized service, which manages the access to each content and the respective keys.

The specification of the system is not available and the implementation is closed source. Thus, the functionalities and the implementation cannot be completely examined and compared to the goals of this book. The available documentation of the system describes that a MPEG-21 based file format is used for the packaging of the content and the content is transferred in the form of a Digital Item. The MPEG-21 REL is also applied to express the rights and to control the governance. The author can grant the rights of reading, listening, viewing or printing to other users. Furthermore, the system allows to set a limitation in time or to define how often the user may execute the rights on the content. The SmartRM system also applies the TPM in the system for the content protection and exchange. There is also a statement which declares that the server performs a Remote Attestation of the client to ensure the trustworthiness of the client. Nevertheless, no details about the realizations of these functionalities are available.

There are two implementations of the system available: a Firefox plug-in and a standalone version for the Macintosh operating systems. The Firefox

3.3. COMPARISON WITH OTHER SYSTEMS 75

plug-in is the central component of the system, which is available for the most operating systems. It is a part of the Firefox Internet browser [18] and can be used for the creation and the accessing of governed content. The plug-in also contains a user management to contact other users similar to messenger applications. The standalone version for the Macintosh operating system provides the identical features as the browser plug-in. Standalone versions for other operating systems are under development.

Compared to the concept of this book, the major goal of the SmartRM system is the protection and also the governance of content. The goal of protecting content is also investigated in this book, however, the governance is not desired. The concept of this book lets it in the responsibility of the user to ensure the correct usage and protection of the exchanged content.

Furthermore, the application of the TPM for the protection is also shared in this book. The SmartRM system uses, however, a centralized server for the key and access management, which differs from the goals of this book. This book concentrates on the protection of the confidentiality of content using a decentralized architecture. A central service for the key management is thus not required. Instead of this, the file format was extended in such a way, which allows a direct transmission of content between users.

3.3.1.2 Key management in MPEG-21 IPMP

The paper [92] presents several methods for the content protection and key management based on the MPEG-21 standards. They identified several use cases for DRM systems and propose methods for their realization using the standards in MPEG-21. Examples of these use cases are the download, the distribution and the domain management of users or devices. The authors compare three representatives systems (MPEG-21, Open Mobile Alliance and Digital Media Project) regarding their key and license management. The result of this comparison shows that all systems contain minimal specifications regarding the realization of these security aspects.

For this reason, they propose methods for the realization of these security aspects. They developed the methods on the basis of the MPEG-21 framework and present protocols for each identified use case. Furthermore, they differentiate in several methods of transportation of the encryption key of the content. The transportation of this key can be either separated of the content or together with the content. For the joint transportation of the key, they apply the MPEG-21 IPMP standard and integrate the license and the key information within the resource of an Item.

The paper presents generalized methods for the key and license management using the MPEG-21 IPMP standard. They do not consider the application of Trusted Computing and the required modifications to support this technology. This book concentrates on this scenario and presents a method to support Trusted Computing in MPEG-21. Furthermore, the paper proposes the transportation of the key within the resource of an Item. This book shows that this can be problematic in combination with Digital Signatures and presents another possibility, which uses the MPEG-21 DID to integrate this information.

3.3.1.3 Other proposals

There are several other proposals, which work in that area, but are not directly comparable to the proposal in this book.

On implementing MPEG-21 IPMP The paper [98] describes several methods of implementing the MPEG-21 IPMP standard to realize a flexible and active management of IPMP tools. It presents an implementation of the standard, which uses the MPEG-21 REL as interface to the tools of the IPMP standard. Within the implementation it also describes the architecture of a key infrastructure for the exchange of the cryptographic keys. The presented key infrastructure, however, only concentrates on the IPMP standard and the exchange of tools in a centralized architecture. It does not consider other standards or the Trusted Computing technology in a decentralized structure.

Evaluating the usability of usage controls in electronic collaboration Another concept is described in [43], which uses Trusted Computing to enforce the usage control of applications. The authors focus on the usage restrictions of Portable Document Format (PDF) documents and show an implementation based on such PDF documents. The paper wants to ensure that the usage information in a PDF document, like the prohibition of printing, is enforced by a secure basis using the TPM. They present a server and client implementations, which use policy files on the basis of the ODRL to

3.3. COMPARISON WITH OTHER SYSTEMS

describe and exchange rights information about the usage of the documents. The client requires a TPM and uses keys stored in the TPM to protect and exchange these policy files. Furthermore, the proposal uses the UCLinux architecture [84] to protect the operating system using measurements and enables the remote attestation of platforms. The paper concentrates on the usage control and enforcement of proprietary policy files using Trusted Computing and does not provide an extensible and interoperable approach to exchange confidential content. The paper shows a method for protecting PDF documents, but does not describe the realization for other types of content. This book presents a concept for any type of content and does not focus on the enforcement of rights expressions. Furthermore, the application of the MPEG-21 framework provides an interoperable and extensible basis for the support of upcoming formats or functions.

Implementing trusted terminals with a TPM and SITDRM Similar to the previous paper, the authors in [99] present a trusted terminal, which applies Trusted Computing to protect the privacy of a user in a limited environment. The MPEG-21 REL is used to declare whether a remote party is allowed to access the data in the terminal. The client parses the licenses and interprets them for the authorization of the remote parties. To ensure a secure storage and correct processing of the licenses, they use the TPM as a security basis. The TPM performs the measurement and the attestation of the operating system. The paper focuses on the protection of the integrity of the platform and the enforcement of the licenses in a remote terminal. This is not in the scope of this book, which shows a method of key management using standardized formats and metadata.

3.3.2 Timestamps in digital signatures

The main goal in this part is the application of TPM-based timestamps within digital signatures declared in XML. It can be divided into the two principal aspects for the comparison with other proposals. The first aspect is the application of tickstamps created by the TPM and the other aspect is the representation of timestamps in signatures using XML.

3.3.2.1 Applications of tickstamps

Remote attestation on legacy operating systems with TPM The existing concepts use the tickstamp functionality of the TPM only to improve the remote attestation of other platforms. One example is [95], which describes another method for the remote attestation for legacy platforms using the tickstamp function of the TPM. The method wants to detect a tampered platform by verifying the memory of a remote program using checksums. The timing of this verification is an important indicator for the integrity of the program. The tickstamp in the TPM is used to improve this type of verification, because the TPM provides a security basis to perform the calculation of the time directly on the remote platform. The proposal does not require an absolute time and does not deal with signatures based on XML in the concept and thus differs from the concept in this book.

Improving the scalability of platform attestation The paper [100] presents several methods to improve the scalability of the remote attestation. One method uses tickstamps to create a token using a protected key stored in the TPM. This token can then be used for the remote attestation to another party. This method uses the tickstamp counter mainly as a kind of session to prove that the integrity of the platform did not change as long as the session is valid. The presented method also does not deal with digital signatures or the representation of the tickstamps in XML.

3.3.2.2 Representation of timestamps

The representation and creation of timestamps is another domain which is developed and improved by many researchers. In particular, the topic of representation of timestamps in XML is relevant for the comparison to the concept of this book. In [108] the authors describe a method of mapping the timestamps in the available binary format to the XML format. They developed a XML structure, which is a proposal for the development of a representation of timestamps and a timestamp protocol in XML. They considered several types of timestamps and developed a XML representation for each type. Furthermore, they present protocols using XML for the creation of these timestamps. The paper does not deal with Trusted Computing and

3.3. COMPARISON WITH OTHER SYSTEMS

the representation of the tickstamps in XML. This is shown in this book, which can be understood as an extension of this paper.

3.3.3 User authentication

For the authentication of users, this book uses the OpenID system. The TPM is used to improve the security of the authentication to the OpenID Provider using a plug-in of the Firefox browser. There are several plug-ins for the Firefox browser, which enhance the user experience or security aspects of the authentication. A common functionality is the storage of the passwords in the browser using a master password, which eases the authentication for the user, because the browser can login the user automatically after the authentication with the master password. This functionality and the plug-ins, which provide this functionality are not explained in this section, because they do not replace the authentication mechanism and just improve the user experience. The following plug-ins and concept are compared regarding their enhancement in security.

3.3.3.1 VeriSign's OpenID SeatBelt Plug-in

SeatBelt [30] is a plug-in for the Firefox browser, which was developed by VeriSign. It is a small plug-in, which enhances the user experience of the OpenID authentication and prevents basic phishing attacks. The enhancement of the user experience is not relevant regarding security aspects. The phishing attacks are prevented in the plug-in by a list of trusted OpenID Providers, which is stored in the client. When the user wants to login to a Relaying Party, the plug-in verifies if the URL, where the browser is redirected to, belongs to OpenID Provider in the list. If the URL is not found, the user is warned and the authentication is prevented.

The plug-in enables the user to view the list of OpenID Providers and to insert a new Provider or to remove an existing one. The plug-in provides a basic functionality to prevent phishing attacks in OpenID, but does not enhance the authentication mechanism. Most sites still use the unsafe method of the password authentication, which should be replaced by more secure authentication method.

3.3.3.2 Other proposals

There are a high volume of proposals which improve the security of the OpenID authentication. The following concepts are the most relevant for this book, which show the security vulnerability of the OpenID specification and other solutions to resolve them.

A new anti-phishing method in OpenID The authors in [85] improve OpenID resistance against phishing attacks by using a two way authentication over separate communication channels. Before the user authenticates to the OpenID Provider, he verifies the authenticity of the Provider with a shared secret. For this purpose, the registration of the user is extended. When the user registers, the Provider stores the shared secret in the client and the user enters a personal message in the server. After that, when the user wants to authenticate at the Provider, the user transmits the shared secret to the Provider. If the secret is valid, the Provider shows the personal message. The user verifies the personal message to determine that he is connected to the same Provider as during the registration. This approach is a possibility of preventing phishing attacks to the server, which has no additional requirements on the client side. It does, however, not replace the password authentication and does not apply secure hardware for the protection of the identity of the user.

Preventing identity theft with electronic identity cards and the TPM In the paper [82], the authors describe a method to protect an identity of a user using the TPM, OpenID and electronic identity cards. The aim is to protect the identity of a user in the Internet, which is provided by the electronic identity cards. The author uses a key stored in the TPM to bind the identity to the platform of the user. The paper describes a part of the authentication mechanism shown in this book, but the authors focus on the application of the electronic identity cards. It does not provide information about the protocols, components and their realization, which is required in an elaborated and applicable solution.

3.4 Developed concepts

This section shows three concepts, which enhance the security in different areas of a content management system. The aim is to develop a system, which allows the user of the platform to benefit of the security features the TPM provides. The design principle is to mainly rely on a peer-to-peer architecture, which uses the same level for the users. This increases the reliability, because no sophisticated centralized infrastructure is required.

The TPM uses a PKI structure, the PrivacyCA, for the verification of the AIK keys. This infrastructure is needed to support this verification. The Direct Anonymous Attestation (DAA) [42] is an alternative method to perform this verification in a peer-to-peer architecture, but there are no elaborated implementations of the protocol available to apply it practically in complex systems. For this reason, the PrivacyCA is used in this book as standard verification method. It can, however, be replaced with the DAA algorithm as desired, because both methods provide the verification of AIK keys.

The three developed concepts are presented in the following sections. The first concept presents the secure storage of confidential data on a platform as well as the secure transmission of content. After that, the TPM is used for the creation and application of qualified timestamps, which are integrated in signatures. The last concept presents an enhanced user authentication in OpenID.

3.4.1 Secure content storage and transmission

The aim of the concept is to protect the confidentiality of content with the application of the TPM in the MPEG-21 framework. This can be realized, if the content is securely stored within a platform and the transmission between platforms is protected. These two aspects are considered on the application level using the MPEG-21 framework as a basis for interoperability. For the protection of content, digital signature and encryption are required to achieve a comprehensive protection. The following section presents a method for the integration of digital signatures into the MPEG-21 framework.

82   CHAPTER 3. PROTECTION USING TRUSTED COMPUTING

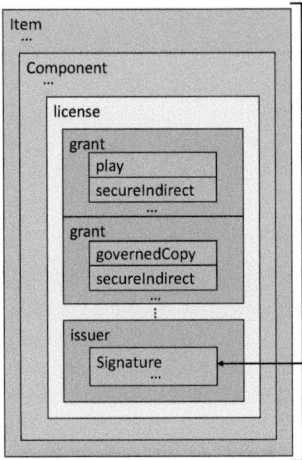

Figure 3.9: Encapsulated signature within an Item

3.4.1.1   Digital signatures

A digital signature enables the verification of authenticity, integrity and verifiability of a content. An author signs a content to ensure that the content cannot be modified maliciously in his name. As already mentioned in section 2.4.2.10, there are several possibilities for the integration of signatures in the MPEG-21 standards. A typical file conform to the MPEG-21 standards packages several Items in a defined structure. Generally, a signature can be thus applied to each Item or to the whole file. The application and the embedding of a signature in an Item are shown schematically in figure 3.9.

It depicts a structural representation of some of the XML elements in an Item. The different capitalization originates from different specifications in the respective standards. Among other elements, the *Item* contains a *Component* element, which in turn contains a *license* element. This license is according to the REL specification and comprises several *grant* elements, which assign rights to users. The last element in the *license* is the *issuer*, which contains the signature of the author. The supported method of representation of a signature in the REL standard is the XMLDSig standard [50].

3.4. DEVELOPED CONCEPTS

A signature can protect an Item completely or only parts of it. The protection of a whole Item is depicted in the figure using the black arrows. The encapsulated signature signs all elements within the Item besides one exception, which is explained later. The figure also shows that the *grant* element contains also the *secureIndirect* element. This element references to the binary resource in the file format using a hash. When the file is compiled, the hash is calculated over the resource and embedded in the *secureIndirect* before the signature is created. This hash value links the resource to the signature and ensures the integrity of the content during the distribution.

The protection of a whole file comprising several Items is realized with another signature, which needs to be embedded in a superior level of the Items. This signature is embedded below the root *DIDL* element and signs all Items with their metadata. This includes the *licenses* with the *secureIndirect* elements, which protect the integrity of the respective content.

The user requires an asymmetric signing key pair to create the signature. This key pair has to be created before the content can be signed. The TPM can be used for the key generation and the storage using a Storage Key. As the signing key is encrypted with the Storage Key, it can be stored externally on any storage device. When a signature is created, the key is loaded into the TPM with the password of the Storage key. An AIK with a PrivacyCA allows to verify that the signing key is protected by the TPM.

These signatures protect the content of modifications and should remain intact during the whole distribution period to attribute the Item to the author.

3.4.1.2 Content storage

Confidentiality of content can be achieved using the MPEG-21 IPMP standard, which defines a method to embed protection information within the MPEG-21 DID. Generally, the IPMP standard defines the notion of a tool which represents any cryptographic algorithm that provides one or more security services. The IPMP standard enables the declaration of such an IPMP tool and its description, e.g. the algorithm and the location of its implementation. To protect the confidentiality of content, a tool is defined, which represents an encryption algorithm. This IPMP tool contains all required information about the type of algorithm and its parameters. The

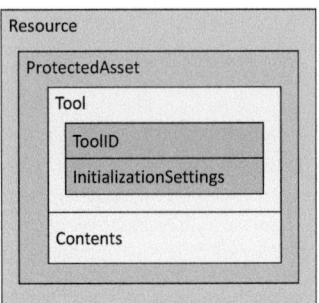

Figure 3.10: Content encryption with MPEG-21 IPMP

tool can be integrated on the level in the DID hierarchy, which is required to ensure the security of the content. The lowest level is the encryption of the content itself, while the metadata in the Item remains unencrypted. A higher level is the encryption of the whole Item, which ensures that only the recipient can decrypt and interpret the metadata in the Item. The level of encryption is thus application dependent and can be chosen as required.

In this book, the level of encryption is chosen on the lowest level, i.e. only the content is encrypted and the unencrypted metadata allows third parties to identify and categorize the content. In this case, the IPMP tool refers only to the resource in the DID. The optimal integration of the declaration of the tool is thus in the *Resource* element of an *Item* element. Figure 3.10 shows this integration schematically.

The surrounding *Resource* element in gray is used as defined in the DID. The original resource within this element is replaced by the IPMP *ProtectedAsset* element. The attributes in the *Resources* element are changed accordingly to reflect that the resource is encrypted using IPMP. The *ProtectedAsset* element defines an IPMP tool, which describes the encryption of the content. The *ToolID* element contains the identifier of the used encryption algorithm, which informs the recipient about the method of encryption. Typically, symmetric encryption algorithms are used for efficiency reasons. The *InitializationSettings* element specifies values, which the selected algorithm requires as parameters for the execution of the algorithm. The original resource is encrypted and embedded in the *Contents* element. This element

3.4. DEVELOPED CONCEPTS

also defines the type of the content before its encryption.

The symmetric keys for the encryption can be generated by a software key generator or the TPM. The TPM contains a key generator, which uses the internal random number generator to generate strong keys. After the encryption, the key can also be stored in the TPM, which binds the key to the platform. As the memory of the TPM is limited, the key is exported using a Storage Key in the key hierarchy. The user has to specify a password, which uses the TPM for the exportation of the key. This password is used to authenticate the user to protect the key against misuse. The key can be also bound to the platform state using the sealing functionality of the TPM. This is an independent issue and not considered in this book, because it requires a special operating system, which makes use of the platform integrity features of the TPM.

3.4.1.3 Transmission of content

The transmission of content is an integral issue in content management. A transmission is performed, when the content is transferred between different users or several platforms.

On a single platform, several users can transmit their content between each other. In this case, it is sufficient either to share the key between the users or to re-encrypt the content for another user. Using the protection mechanism as described in the previous section, the sharing of the key can be realized with the sharing of the password, which is required to load the key into the TPM. This password has to be revealed to the authorized users. Alternatively, the content can be re-encrypted, if a permanent sharing of the password is a security risk. A key can be created, which is only shared temporarily between the sender and the recipient. After the generation of this key, the content is re-encrypted with it. The encrypted content is transferred to the recipient, which can then decrypt the content with the shared key. The recipient may then again re-encrypt the content with a new key, which is not shared with another party. The shared key and the corresponding content can then be deleted. This method is more complex, but increases the security as the shared key is only required temporarily. Another advantage is that it does not require external parties for the transmission. This method is, however, only applicable in a single platform and the security significantly

CHAPTER 3. PROTECTION USING TRUSTED COMPUTING

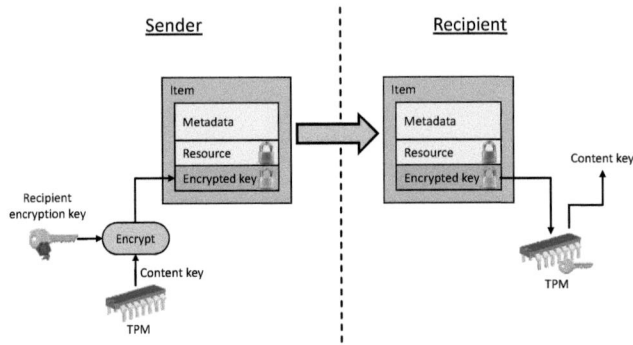

Figure 3.11: Method for key exchange within an Item

depends on the protected exchange of the encryption key. This can lead to almost the same efforts, which is required for the transmission between several platforms. So this method is only beneficial in special use cases.

The comprehensive approach is the transmission of content between several platforms. This can be also generally used for the transmission of content within a single platform, because it provides a secure method to exchange the encryption key. The aim for this method is to develop a solution for the secure transmission of the encryption key without modifying the operating system or the method of transmission. This is achieved by embedding the content key into the MPEG-21 metadata of an Item. This method is shown schematically in figure 3.11.

Before the transmission of the Item to the recipient, the sender extends the Item with an encrypted key, which is derived from the content key. If the content is stored outside of the TPM, the content key is loaded into the TPM using the respective Storage Key and extracted from the TPM. After that, the application encrypts the content key with the encryption key of the recipient. This encryption key is the public part of an asymmetric key pair, whose private part is bound to the TPM of the recipient. This ensures that the encrypted key can only be decrypted within the TPM of the recipient. The encryption key has to be transferred to the sender before the transmission together with an AIK certificate. This certificate proves that

3.4. DEVELOPED CONCEPTS

the key originates from an authentic TPM. In the next step, the encrypted key is embedded into the Item as additional encapsulated metadata.

In the Item, both the resource and the encapsulated key are encrypted, which ensures the confidentiality of the content. As a result, the Item may be transferred with any arbitrary method or protocol to the recipient. After the transfer, the recipient extracts the encrypted key from the Item and uses the private part of the encryption key in the TPM to decrypt the content key. This key enables the user to decrypt the resource and to access the content.

This is a schematic overview of the functionality. The next paragraphs show the individual steps of the method and the integration in MPEG-21 in detail.

Prerequisites To transmit content with the presented method, the sender requires to obtain the public part of the recipient's encryption key. Together with the key, he should get certificates from the recipient, which allow the verification of the authenticity of the key. The recipient uses his TPM to create the encryption key and stores the private part of the key within the TPM. This enables the TPM to sign the public part of the key with a previously created AIK. The result is a certificate, which states that the key was created by the TPM and remains protected. The AIK in turn is signed and certified by a PrivacyCA, which ensures that the AIK is authentic. The recipient has to trust the PrivacyCA or one of its superior certification authorities in a hierarchical PKI.

The method of how to obtain the encryption key of the recipient with its certificates, is not prescribed in this book. Generally, the sender requires a functionality to select other users and to retrieve their respective encryption keys. This functionality can be performed manually or it can be a part of an overall user management. The sender needs to be able to identify the user and its certificates to verify that the encryption key belongs to the correct user. An example is a central service, which performs the user management and provides an interface to obtain the public part of the encryption key of other users. The sender could contact this service, select a user as recipient and retrieve his encryption key.

After the user has obtained the encryption key, he can encrypt the content key and embed it into an Item specified by MPEG-21 DID.

Integration in MPEG-21 The MPEG-21 DID defines Items as a superior structure for a content. It comprises the resource and the metadata into a single asset, which contains information about the content and its distribution. The distribution is governed for example with the MPEG-21 REL. As shown in section 2.4.2.5, the REL also supports use cases, where content is shared without restriction between an unlimited amount of users. The permanent re-distribution is an integral aspect in the decentralized content management. This issue is even more complex if digital signatures are involved. As shown in section 3.4.1.1, an Item may be signed to ensure authenticity and integrity of the content. A signature preserves the integrity of the Item, which would also hinder the embedding of the encrypted content key for the transmission of a content. The embedded key has to be inserted in such a way that it is ignored by the signature to preserve its validity.

Semantically, the embedded key represents additional descriptive metadata within the Item, which addresses the MPEG-21 DID for the integration of the key. For such a case, the MPEG-21 DID foresees the *Annotation* element, which contains information, about an "identified entity of the model without altering or adding to that entity" [70]. This element can be used to embed the key into the Item, without modifying semantically the resource or the metadata belonging to the resource. To preserve the validity of the signature, the *Annotation* element has to be excluded from the signature. This allows to insert, modify or to remove *Annotation* elements from the Item, while the signatures prove the authenticity and the integrity of the Item. The signature also remains intact when the Item is copied to other Items or aggregated with other Items. This eases the exchange, because this method for the encrypted transmission does not affect the distribution of the content.

This method has, however, a disadvantage, because the same content key is shared with many users. This is a security risk, because the probability of a violation of the secrecy of the key increases per user. To change the content key for every user, the content has to be re-encrypted with a new key. This would, however, invalidate the signature of the content and a new signature has to be created by the sender. In this case, the process for the transmission of content would be almost identical to the process for the release of a content. A re-encryption can be required in application scenarios, where different content keys per user are required. It has to be defined in the

3.4. DEVELOPED CONCEPTS

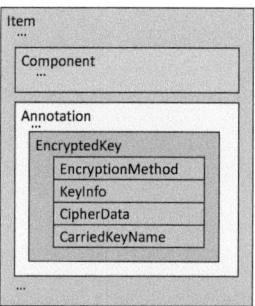

Figure 3.12: Embedding of a key in an *Annotation* element

particular application scenario, whether a re-encryption is preferred over the validity of the original signature. This book considers the case in which a re-encryption is not required and the original signature should be preserved.

The structural integration of the encrypted key in the *Annotation* element is shown in figure 3.12. The *Annotation* element is positioned after the *Component* element within the Item. An Item may have an unlimited amount of *Annotation* elements, which allows to insert multiple keys in an Item. The structure of the *Annotation* element contains an attribute, which allows to specify the content type of the information in the *Annotation*. This enables the recipient to distinguish an *Annotation* transporting an encrypted key from *Annotation* elements containing other information.

Within the *Annotation* element is the *EncryptedKey* element, which was presented in section 3.1.1. The *EncryptedKey* element comprises the embedded key and related identifiers for the keys and the recipient. The recipient is specified as a URI in an attribute of the *EncryptedKey* element. The recipient is the identifier of the user, who is in possession of the required private key.

The inferior *EncryptionMethod* element declares the encryption algorithm, which is used to en- or decrypt the embedded key. As this operation is performed by the TPM, the RSA algorithm is selected in this element. The key used for the encryption of the embedded key is specified in the *KeyInfo* element. This element is based on the XMLDSig standard and can contain the *RetrievalMethod* element, which notifies the recipient that the encrypted key can be obtained from the TPM. The *RetrievalMethod* has the two attributes *Type* and *URI*. The *Type* contains a URI value, which declares the type of the retrieved data. This value is set to a specific identifier to notify the recipient that the key can be retrieved from the TPM. The *URI* attribute specifies an identifier, which allows to locate the key within the persistent storage of TPM. The *CipherData* element contains the encrypted key as binary data. The embedded key is identified with the information in the *CarriedKeyName* element, which allows to distinguish several encrypted keys in an Item.

This structure enables the embedding of an encryption key into an Item. An Item with such an embedded key can be distributed and confidentially transmitted to the recipient. The next section investigates two methods for the distribution of such Items.

3.4.1.4 Distribution and addressing of users

The distribution of the encrypted Items can be categorized in two methods: the direct transmission and the transfer over a trusted third party. The direct transfer is the straightforward approach, in which the sender encrypts the content and transmits it to the recipient. A transfer over a trusted third party may be required if the sender wants to transmit a single content to a defined group of people. In this case, the recipient is not a single user, but a group of users. Depending on the size of the group, it would be inefficient to encrypt the content key multiple times for all users in the group. The sender could also use group keys, but this would increase the effort in the key management. A trusted third party can reduce the efforts by interacting as an agent between the users. The concept and realization of these two methods are shown in the following paragraphs.

Direct transmission The encrypted content can be transmitted directly to the recipient. As the content is encrypted, it can be transferred with any method or protocol. This can be for example via portable devices, e-mail or directly from application to application. The recipient is either a single user or a limited group of users. For each user, the sender can embed a separate encrypted key into the Item. This allows to distribute and share a single

3.4. DEVELOPED CONCEPTS

file with multiple users. Each recipient can distinguish the encrypted keys with the recipient attribute of the *EncryptedKey* element. This allows the recipient to determine, if the associated key is directed to him. Although this method is inefficient if the sender wants to address a large group of users or if the particular users are unknown to the sender. This can be improved with the introduction of an intermediate trusted party, which is explained in the next paragraph.

Trusted third party A trusted third party can act as an intermediate agent for the distribution of content. This third party is aware of the format and can parse and process the available metadata of the Item. A sender can transmit the content to the third party, which then distributes the content autonomously to the respective users. This increases the efficiency in scenarios, where a sender wants to share a content with a large group of users. To transmit the content to the third party, the sender can use the same encryption mechanism as for the direct transmission. The sender requires the public key of the third party to encrypt the content key. The public key has to be verifiable to ensure the authenticity of the third party. After the transfer, the third party can decrypt the content key and has thus access to the content. For this reason, the third party has to be trustworthy to preserve the confidentiality of the content. This method has the advantage that the third party can act as a centralized service, which distributes the content to the selected users.

The sender chooses the desired recipients before the transfer to the server using the MPEG-21 REL. The REL provides several methods, which allow the sender to select a specific group of users. One example is the *Identity-Holder* element, which contains an identifier to select specific users or devices. The third party uses this information to determine if a user may obtain a content. For this task, a user management is required, which allows the third party to verify the authenticity of a user. When the user is authentic and the access to a content is granted, the third party transmits the content to the user. It can use the same method with an encrypted key as for the direct transmission. This ensures the confidentiality of the content and minimizes efforts in the implementation.

The third party can provide this service as long as necessary for the respective content. It works independent of the sender and can be thus more reliable and highly available for the recipients. It may also adopt if changes in the recipients occur, for example a user joins a specific group after the sender transferred the content to the third party. The third party can automatically verify this change and transmit the content to the new user without another negotiation with the sender.

3.4.1.5 Summary

The presented method enables the secure storage and the exchange of confidential content with two or more users. The key management of the encrypted content is decentralized and relies on the responsibility of the users. The embedding of the encrypted key into the Item eases the exchange of the content, because any method for the transmission can be applied. No changes in the underlying operating system or external communication is required. The applications on both sides, the sender and the receiver, have to be implemented conform to a common file and metadata format. The MPEG-21 framework provides these technologies as a good basis for the interoperability on the application level.

3.4.2 Timestamps in digital signatures

Digital signatures ensure authenticity, integrity and verifiability of content. The integration of timestamps enhances signatures, because it allows to verify the point in time when the signature was created. In section 3.1.4.6, the functionality and the protocol for the creation of a TPM-timestamp using the tick counter of the TPM was presented. This section shows the XML representation of such a timestamp and its integration in signatures.

The values of a TPM-timestamp are shown in figure 3.13. The Reference-Info value specifies a reference to the document, which is timestamped. The TSA-timestamp is the traditional timestamp created by the TSA. The three tickstamps and the AIK credentials are the new elements, which are created by the TPM. These values have to be mapped to a representation in XML and integrated into signatures. The XAdES standard already contains elements, which can represent timestamps within signatures. To be compliant to this standard, the elements defined in XAdES were used as a basis for the integration of the additional values from the TPM.

3.4. DEVELOPED CONCEPTS

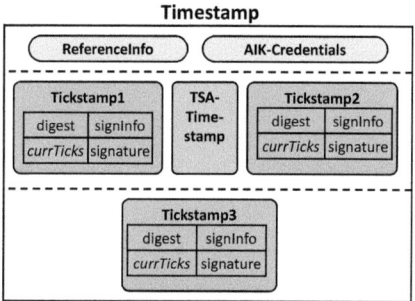

Figure 3.13: Timestamp created by the TPM

The central type for the representation of a timestamp in XAdES is the *GenericTimeStampType*. As the TPM also creates a timestamp, the *GenericTimeStampType* is derived to create a new TPM-specific type of a timestamp. This derivation is called *GenericTimeStampExtensionType* in this book. From this generic type, the specific type for the TPM-timestamp is created and named *TPMTimeStamp* with the type *TPMTimeStampType*. The next sections show these types and the mapping of the values to the *GenericTimeStampType*.

3.4.2.1 GenericTimeStampExtensionType

In the XAdES standard, the *GenericTimeStampType* is the basis of all timestamps. For particular use cases, the type is restricted to the specific type of timestamp, which is required for the use case. To integrate the TPM-timestamp in XAdES, the *GenericTimeStampType* has to be extended to support the additional values. The *GenericTimeStampExtensionType* is the proposed extended type, which is shown in figure 3.14. The figure was created with the software Altova XMLSpy [35].

The former *GenericTimeStampType* was extended with two elements marked in red: the *TickStamp* and the *AikCredentials*. These elements are optional, so the backward-compatibility is preserved. The *GenericTimeStampExtensionType* can transparently replace the old type without interference to the supported use cases. The *AikCredentials* element contains the

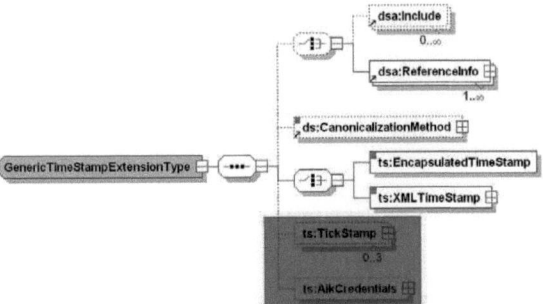

Figure 3.14: The GenericTimeStampExtensionType

AIK credentials in a format, which is compliant to the X.509 standard [47]. The XML representation for such a certificate is the *X509DataType*, which is standardized in the XMLDSig standard.

The *TickStamp* element can appear up to three times and contains the tickstamps, which were explained in section 3.1.4.8. Two of these tickstamps are required to link the tick counter of the TPM to an universal time and the third tickstamp finalizes the TPM-timestamp over the document. The other elements are used as they are defined in the XAdES standard to keep the backward compatibility to the current timestamps.

3.4.2.2 TPMTimeStampType

In the XAdES standard the concrete timestamp types are derived from the abstract *GenericTimeStampType*. To be compliant to this scheme, a new type, the *TPMTimeStampType* is introduced, which is a restriction of the *GenericTimeStampType*. The figure 3.15 shows the structure of the *TPMTimeStampType* and its mapping to the values of the TPM-timestamp.

The difference to the *GenericTimeStampExtensionType* is that the *TickStamp* and *AikCredentials* elements are not optional in each instance of the *TPMTimeStampType*. The *AikCredentials* has to be present exactly one time and exactly three instances of the *TickStamp* elements are required.

To specify the timestamped document, the *Include* element or the *Refer-*

3.4. DEVELOPED CONCEPTS

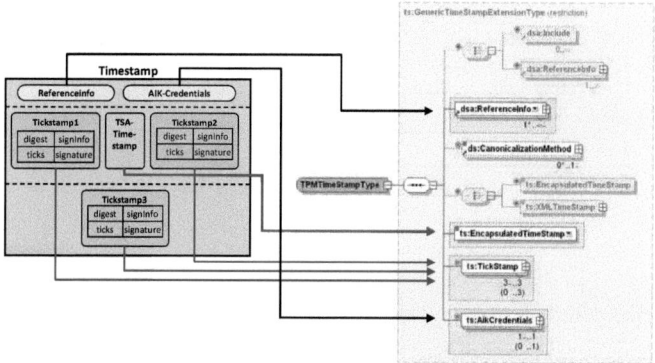

Figure 3.15: The *TPMTimeStampType* and its mapping to the TPM-timestamp

enceInfo element can be used. The choice between the two elements depends on the use case and the document to timestamp. In this book, the *Include* element is removed, because its complexity in the implementation is higher. The *ReferenceInfo* element is kept to directly embed the hash value of the document within the element. The detailed values within the *TickStamp* element are shown in the next section.

3.4.2.3 Tickstamp

The XML-representation and the mapping of a tickstamp is shown in figure 3.16.

Neither the XMLDSig nor the XAdES standard contain a structure suitable for embedding the values of a tickstamp, thus necessitating a newly developed structure. A tickstamp comprises four elements: digest, signInfo, currTicks, and signature.

The digest of the tickstamp is mapped to the *digestToStamp* element. This element is optional, because it is not required for the third tickstamp. The third tickstamp contains the digest over the document, which is already specified in the *ReferenceInfo* element of the *TPMTimeStampType*. The *SignInfo* element contains the values, which are created by the TPM during

96   CHAPTER 3. PROTECTION USING TRUSTED COMPUTING

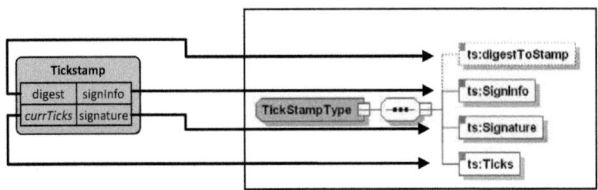

Figure 3.16: The *TickStampType* and its mapping to the tickstamp

the tickstamp operation. This data is required for the verification of the signature, and is thus embedded as is. Similar to the signInfo, the currTicks value is created during the tickstamp operation and embedded as binary value in the *Ticks* element. These values can also be separated, if desired. The signature value is mapped to the *Signature* element and contains the resulting value of the signature operation.

The *TickStampType* elements also have another attribute, which allows the identification of the tickstamp within the TPM-timestamp. This attribute can be the number one, two or three depending on the respective tickstamp. All four values, digest, signInfo, currTicks and signature, are represented as binary values in XML with the base64Binary-Type. Although signInfo and currTicks are composites of several single values, they are kept as one binary value, because this eases the verification of the signature. These values are returned from the TPM in this form and their preservation facilitates their processing.

3.4.2.4   Verification of the timestamp

The previous sections presented the mapping of the TPM-timestamp with a XML structure based on the XAdES standard. The recipient of such a timestamp has to verify the values and the signatures to determine if the timestamp is valid. This verification consists of several steps, which must be executed to obtain the result.

First, the three tickstamps themselves are validated to ensure their integrity. To accomplish this, the *SignInfo* element is verified by comparing the value with the values in *digestToStamp* and *Ticks*. Then, the signature

3.4. DEVELOPED CONCEPTS

can be decrypted with the public key of the AIK. This key is transmitted in the *AIKCredentials* element as part of the certificate. Furthermore, the hash value of the *SignInfo* value has to be calculated and compared to the decrypted signature value. If the values are equal, then the tickstamp is valid.

In addition to the tickstamps, the TSA-timestamp and the AIK have to be verified. The TSA-timestamp can be validated as a normal signature with the public key of the TSA. The public key of the TSA must be authentic and trusted, e.g. by using a trusted certificate. The AIK is validated with a PrivacyCA, the DAA, or other means to guarantee that the AIK is from an authentic TPM. If all verifications are successful, the TPM-timestamp is valid. The resulting timing is determined with a specific precision depending on the distance between the first two tickstamps.

3.4.2.5 Integration of the TPM-timestamp in signatures

The developed TPM-timestamp enables the user to prove that the timestamped document existed at a certain point in time. The timestamp can be either stored separately or integrated into the document. To prove authenticity and integrity of the document, a separate signature from the author or publisher is required. Usually the timestamp is integrated in such a signature to achieve a comprehensive protection of the document. The following sections show methods of integration of the presented TPM-timestamp in the XMLDSig and XAdES standards.

XMLDSig XMLDSig is the most widely-used standard for the representation of signatures in XML. The XMLDSig standard specifies an *Object* element, which can contain any extensions to the signature like timestamps. The extensions are embedded with a *SignatureProperty* element, which declares an identifier for the extension and a target in its attributes. The target is a reference to the element the extension belongs to. Figure 3.17 shows the most important element as an example of a signature with an integrated *TPMTimeStamp* element. The *TPMTimeStamp* is marked in blue.

The elements in the *Object* element are not automatically included in the creation of the signature and, therefore, not protected. The signature must include the timestamp to ensure the timestamp remains attached to

```
<Signature Id="SignatureAuthor" ...>
    <SignedInfo>
        ...
        <Reference URI="http://www.w3.org/TR/xml-stylesheet/">
            ...
        </Reference>
        <Reference URI="#MyTimeStamp" Type="http://www.w3.org/2000/09/xmldsig#SignatureProperties">
            ...
        </Reference>
    </SignedInfo>
    ...
    <Object>
        <SignatureProperties>
            <SignatureProperty Id="MyTimeStamp" Target="#SignatureAuthor">
                <TPMTimeStamp>
                    ...
                </TPMTimeStamp>
            </SignatureProperty>
        </SignatureProperties>
    </Object>
</Signature>
```

Figure 3.17: Example of integration in XMLDSig

the document. Accordingly, an additional *Reference* in the *SignedInfo* needs to be added in the signature, which is marked in yellow in the figure. In the XML Signature Properties [53] standard, several extensions in the *Object* element are recommended, but the integration of timestamps is not foreseen. To achieve an interoperable integration of timestamps in XMLDSig, a recommendation could be added to this standard.

XAdES The XAdES standard supports timestamps for specific use cases and defines their integration. As XAdES was used as a basis in the developed proposal, the *TPMTimeStampType* can directly replace the existing timestamps. Another advantage of the proposal is that the existing timestamps in the standard can also be realized with the TPM. For example, the existing *AllDataObjectsTimeStamp* can also be created by the TPM. This completes the backward-compatibility and enhances the integration in the existing solutions.

3.4.2.6 Example

Figure 3.18 shows a condensed example of a signature with a timestamp created by the TPM. The namespace of the elements can be seen in the prefixes of the elements. The "ts" prefix refers to the new created element

3.4. DEVELOPED CONCEPTS

```
<Signature xmlns="http://www.w3.org/2000/09/xmldsig#" Id="MySignature">
    <SignedInfo>
        <Reference URI="#MyTPMTimestamp">...</Reference> ...
    </SignedInfo>
    ...
    <Object>
        <SignatureProperties>
            <SignatureProperty Id="MyTPMTimestamp" Target="#MySignature">
                <ts:TPMTimestamp xmlns:ds="http://www.w3.org/2000/09/xmldsig#"
                    xmlns:dsa="http://uri.etsi.org/01903/v1.3.2#"
                    xmlns:ts="TPMTimestamp-NS">
                    <dsa:ReferenceInfo>
                        <ds:DigestMethod Algorithm="..."/>
                        <ds:DigestValue>/LAdIiasdSa2LaKna9aj12sdnkAC8a&</ds:DigestValue>
                    </dsa:ReferenceInfo>
                    <ts:EncapsulatedTimestamp>OANMA.....</ts:EncapsulatedTimestamp>
                    <ts:TickStamp number="1">
                        <ts:digestToStamp>PD2ALMON9T....</ts:digestToStamp>
                        <ts:SignInfo>OXM7XC1BZ....</ts:SignInfo>
                        <ts:Signature>LA9lANS2....</ts:Signature>
                        <ts:Ticks>WKSVMQL72A...</ts:Ticks>
                    </ts:TickStamp>
                    <ts:TickStamp number="2">....</ts:TickStamp>
                    <ts:TickStamp number="3">....</ts:TickStamp>
                    <ts:AikCredentials>
                        <ds:X509Certificate>OYMXSLUW....</ds:X509Certificate>
                    </ts:AikCredentials>
                </ts:TPMTimestamp>
            </SignatureProperty>
        </SignatureProperties>
    </Object>
</Signature>
```

Figure 3.18: Example of a XMLDSig signature with a TPM-timestamp

for the TPM-timestamp. The elements with the prefix "dsa" are from the XAdES standard and the remaining elements are specified in XMLDSig.

3.4.2.7 Summary

The usage of the TPM allows the creation of qualified timestamps without a permanent connection to a TSA. The TPM enables the binding of a trusted timestamp from a TSA to a secure counter. The timestamps created by such a counter can be also verified by external parties. The integration of a TPM timestamp into the XML standards for digital signatures is presented. This enables the representation of the TPM timestamps as XML documents, which enhances the interoperable exchange and processing of the timestamps. The representation is based on the XAdES standard and provides compliance to the existing timestamp definitions in the specification. Furthermore, the integration in XML signatures according to the XAdES or the XMLDSig standard was described.

3.4.3 User authentication

This section presents a concept which uses OpenID as a basis for an authentication of users on websites. The authentication process is enhanced with the integration of the TPM into the protocol. The aim is a comprehensive solution, which benefits from the usability of OpenID and enhances the security using the TPM.

3.4.3.1 Overview

The OpenID specification does not define the method for authentication of the user. This gap can be used to seamlessly integrate the TPM into the authentication process. The integration of the TPM may require a modification of the OpenID standard. Modification are generally not desired, because the OpenID standard is already widely deployed and a modification would mean, that all existing implementations become incompatible regarding the modification. This should be prevented if possible.

The authentication of the user is performed between the Provider and the User Agent. This is the central point for improvement, but also the other components have to be considered and integrated in the whole concept.

An OpenID system consists of the Relaying Party, the Provider and the User Agent. The TPM is built into the User Agent and requires a PrivacyCA to certify the keys within the TPM. All these components are shown in figure 3.19 with the connections between them.

The Relaying Party is a website as specified in the OpenID specification. The User Agent is the component between the Provider and the TPM, which serves as connector between them. The User Agent has to be extended with an add-on to support the functionalities of the TPM. This add-on accesses the TPM via the TSS, therefore, also multiple User Agents can use the TPM simultaneously. The add-on is responsible for the authentication and communicates with http requests with the Provider. The User Agent and also the Provider involve the PrivacyCA to request or validate certificates from the TPM.

To authenticate a user, the protocol of the OpenID specification is used and extended. The beginning of the protocol is identical, where the user enters his OpenID identifier in a web form. After its submission, the User Agent

3.4. DEVELOPED CONCEPTS

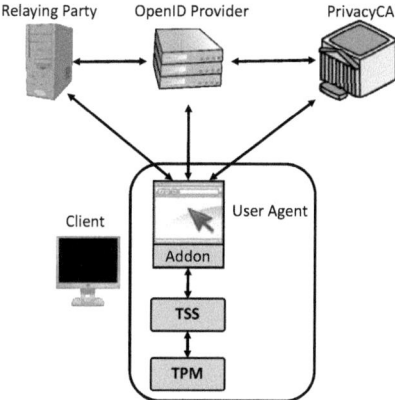

Figure 3.19: Overview of the OpenID system with the TPM

is redirected to the Provider. The add-on is able to recognize this redirection and to initiate a specific protocol which involves the TPM. The add-on accesses the TPM and uses secrets stored in the TPM to authenticate the User to the Provider. The Provider validates the transmitted values and requests additional certificates from the PrivacyCA as required. If the authentication is successful, the Provider redirects the user back to the Relaying Party as specified in the OpenID standard.

The following sections present the details of the concept and the exchanged messages between the components.

3.4.3.2 Components

There are three components involved in the authentication procedure: the TPM, the User Agent, and the OpenID Provider. The Relaying Party does not require any modification and is, therefore, not explained.

TPM - authentication and keys The TPM can store asymmetric keys in a key hierarchy as explained in section 3.1.4.4. The stored keys are encrypted with the SRK or a Storage Key and saved in this encrypted form on a device in the platform. The SRK or Storage Keys are protected with passwords which are set when the key is created. These passwords have to be given each time the key is used for the decryption of inferior keys. If an application wants to use a key for a cryptographic operation, the key has to be loaded and decrypted within the TPM. For the decryption of the key, all keys superior in the hierarchy have to be loaded in the TPM. It starts with the SRK and downwards from level to level the keys are loaded with their passwords into the TPM until the selected key is reached.

The passwords are a method of authentication, because only the user who knows the password is able to load the key into the TPM and to use it. This method is exploited for the authentication in OpenID. Each user posses a Signing Key, whose private part remains in the TPM and is protected in the key hierarchy. The Signing Key is stored encrypted within the User Persistent Storage and the user has to provide the password of the superior Storage Key to use the key. The Signing Key allows the creation of signatures on any data. Such a signature can be used for the authentication to the Provider, because it proves that the user can load the key into the TPM.

The validity of these signatures are verified with an AIK and the PrivacyCA. The TPM signs the Signing Key with an AIK to state that the key is associated and belonging to the TPM. The AIK is certified by the PrivacyCA, which verifies the platform credentials to determine that the AIK belongs to the respective TPM. All these credentials can be transmitted to the Provider, which allows him to validate the authenticity of a signature created by the Signing Key.

User Agent The User Agent consists of the browser and an add-on to that browser. The browser is a common software, which is used for the exchange of information with websites. The add-on enriches the browser with an access to the TPM over the TSS and extends the user interface of the browser. The add-on inserts new functions in the user interface, which allows the user to address the TPM and to perform high-level functions of the TSS. This access to the hardware requires special privileges in the browser, because fully developed browsers implement security mechanisms to prevent malicious software from websites gaining access to private data. The browser has to be configured to grant the hardware access to the add-on.

Furthermore, the add-on is able to recognize the redirection of the User

3.4. DEVELOPED CONCEPTS

Agent to the OpenID Provider. When this occurs, it performs a protocol to authenticate the user. The exchanged messages are transported using the HTTP protocol and via cookies.

OpenID Provider The OpenID Provider receives the information from the add-on and performs the user authentication. To validate the values from the TPM, the Provider uses the PrivacyCA to exchange required certificates. The Provider needs to trust the PrivacyCA to validate the certificates successfully.

3.4.3.3 Use cases

The interaction of the components is divided in three use cases to achieve a concise solution for the management of the users: the registration, the authentication and the deregistration. Each use case implements methods and protocols to achieve the respective functionality for the user management. In the following paragraphs, the three use cases and the integrated improvements are discussed to give an overview of the concept. The next sections describe the protocols in detail.

Registration A user has to be registered in the OpenID Provider to use the OpenID infrastructure for the authentication on websites. In this registration, the user creates a new OpenID identity at the Provider, which he can use later for the authentication. Before the user can register at the Provider, he has to create a Signing Key within the TPM. The Signing Key is encrypted with a Storage Key and stored in the key hierarchy of the TPM. The user enters a password during the creation and the encrypted key is then stored in the User Persistent Storage. The user can initiate the creation of a new key with the add-on. The key may also be created externally with another software and the user may choose to use this key for the authentication in OpenID. The only restriction is that the key must have been created with the same security conditions as with the add-on. In both cases, it must be ensured that the Signing Key is assigned to the user and only the user can provide the necessary passwords to load the key into the TPM.

When the user has a Signing Key within the TPM, he can use the User Agent to connect to the Provider to create an OpenID identity. In a conventional OpenID system, the Provider requests the user to specify a name for his OpenID identity and a password. If the name has not already been taken, the user receives the identifier and is registered. This registration process is extended mainly with the submission of the public part of the Signing Key and the associated certificates for its validation. The Provider validates the certificates to ensure that the key originates from a TPM. The Provider stores the data in a database for the upcoming authentications of the user. After that, the user receives an OpenID identifier and the registration is successful.

Authentication During the registration, the Provider associates the Signing Key and the certificate to the user. This association is exploited in the authentication of the user. The user enters his OpenID identifier at a Relaying Party. The Relaying Party redirects the user to the Provider and the add-on in the User Agents transmits additional data for the authentication. This data is signed by the Signing Key within the TPM. The stored public part of the Signing Key and the certificates allow the Provider to validate the signature. If the signature is authentic, the Provider proved that the same user as in the registration has submitted the signed data. Hence, the user is authentic and is allowed to use the related OpenID identifier.

Deregistration The deregistration of a user completes the user management. In this use case, a registered user account in the Provider is removed and the stored certificates are deleted. After that, the OpenID identifier becomes invalid and cannot be used anymore. It is not required to also remove the Signing Key in the User Persistent Storage. The user can decide to reuse the key for another identity or any other purpose.

3.4.3.4 Registration

This section presents the detailed steps for the registration of a user in the Provider. The aim is to create an association between the OpenID identifier and the Signing Key of the user within the Provider. The steps of the registration are shown in figure 3.20.

The exchanged values and the processing in the components are as follows:

3.4. DEVELOPED CONCEPTS

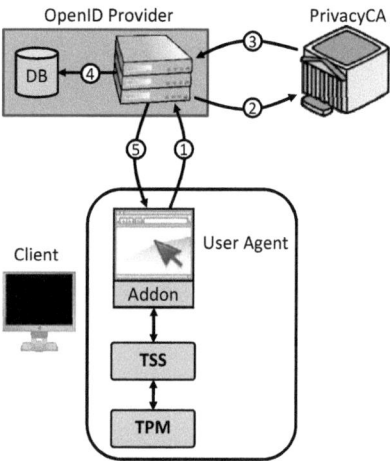

Figure 3.20: Registration of a user at the Provider

1. The user enters the name of the OpenID identifier and the data related to the Signing Key in a web form of the Provider. This data is:

    - AIK certificate
    - UUID of the Signing Key
    - Public part of the Signing Key
    - Signature of the Signing Key with the AIK
    - Signature of the UUID with the Signing Key (optional)

The web form of the Provider needs to provide fields for these values, e.g., the possibility to upload files. The UUID of the Signing Key is the identifier of the key within the TPM. It allows the identification of the correct Signing Key, which has to be loaded into the TPM. The signature of the UUID can be optionally added to ensure that the UUID belongs to the given Signing Key. This is required if the submission of the values is not encrypted to prevent an attacker from modifying the UUID. In comparison to the conventional registration in OpenID, the password is replaced by these values. Hence, the Provider is not aware of the password anymore. When the user has entered all values, the form is submitted to the Provider.

2. The Provider validates the received values. It also validates the AIK certificate with the PrivacyCA to ensure that the certificates belong to an authentic TPM. The PrivacyCA returns the required certificates to the Provider.

3. Upon receipt, the Provider verifies the values of the user. At first, the Provider verifies the signature of the Signing Key with the AIK using the AIK certificate. This ensures that the private part of the Signing Key was created in the TPM and is protected by it. If the signature of the UUID is provided, it is also validated with the public part of the Signing Key.

4. If the validation was successful, the public part of the Signing Key and the UUID are stored in a database (DB) within the Provider. Both values are stored together with the created OpenID identifier of the user. The implementation of the database is up to the Provider and depends on the amount of registered users. Furthermore, the OpenID specific metadata is created, which allows a Relaying Party to discover the Provider.

5. Finally the Provider returns the created OpenID identifier back to the User Agent. The User Agent presents the identifier to the user to inform him.

After this protocol, the user has obtained an OpenID identifier from the Provider. The public part of the Signing Key is transmitted to the OpenID identifier during the registration. This is required to perform the authentication with the Signing Key. Alternatively, the user could also register with a password and specify the Signing Key later on. The password authentication may also be preserved to provide alternative methods for the authentication. This dual approach is more flexible, but the password introduces security risks.

The result after the registration is that the OpenID identifier of the user is linked to the Signing Key in the TPM. The user can then use the identifier to authenticate on any website that supports the OpenID protocol.

3.4. DEVELOPED CONCEPTS

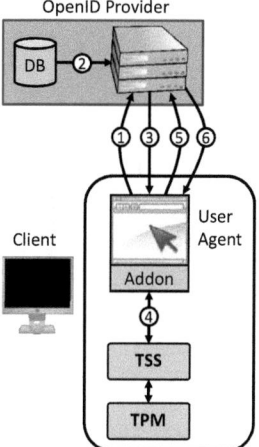

Figure 3.21: Authentication protocol

3.4.3.5 Authentication

The user wants to use the created OpenID identifier to authenticate to a website that supports the OpenID protocol. The first steps with the Relaying Party are identical to the conventional OpenID protocol. The user enters his OpenID identifier to the Relaying Party, which then performs the discovery of the Provider. Afterwards the user is redirected to the Provider, which performs the authentication of the user. The protocol is a challenge-response authentication, which uses a signature to provide an one-way authentication of the user. The protocol and its steps are depicted in figure 3.21.

Each number represents exchange of data between the components. The following information is transmitted and processed in each step:

1. After the redirect of the Relaying Party, the User Agent connects to the Provider. The OpenID identifier is automatically transmitted within the User Agent.

2. The Provider uses the OpenID identifier to locate and load the certificates, keys, and UUID of the user from the database. In this step, the

Provider also verifies if the user is registered. If the OpenID identifier is not registered, the certificates and keys are not stored in the database and the authentication can not be performed. In this case, the Provider can redirect the User Agent to a form, where the user can register.

3. The Provider forwards the UUID of the Signing Key to the add-on in the User Agent. This informs the add-on about the Signing Key, which was used for the registration. This key is also used for the authentication to verify that the current user is the same user as for the registration. Furthermore, the Provider transmits a nonce, which will be signed in the client by the Signing Key within the TPM.

4. The add-on recognizes the received information of the Provider and connects to the TSS. The add-on loads the Signing Key belonging to the received UUID. The user is prompted to enter the password for the key. When the loading of the key was successful, the nonce received from the Provider is signed with the Signing Key.

5. The created signature is transmitted to the Provider. The Provider in turn verifies the signature with the public part of the Signing Key. The public part of Signing Key does not need to be verified, because the key has already been checked during the registration. After the registration, the TPM ensures that the private part of the Signing Key remains within the TPM and the platform. As a result, the Provider knows that the signature was created by the same key which was used for the registration. As the user is the only person in the possession of the private part of the Signing Key, the user is authenticated.

6. The Provider sends the authentication result to the User Agent and redirects him back to the Relaying Party. The Relaying Party verifies the authentication result to determine if the authentication was successful.

The presented protocol is not precise regarding the connection to the TPM. The session management in the TSS allows the add-on to open a connection to the TPM and to keep it open over a longer period of time. When the add-on has started a session, the Session Key is loaded into the TPM and it can be used for several authentications. This enhances the usability, because the password is only required when a new session is started.

3.4. DEVELOPED CONCEPTS

However, the longer the session is kept open, the higher is the probability that an attacker can take over the existing session. This can be achieved, for example, by network intruders or viruses. Therefore, it is more secure to close the session after each authentication. If a higher usability is preferred, the session can be kept open a reasonable period of time, which is the optimum between usability and security for the specific general conditions.

The presented authentication protocol remains compatible with the OpenID specification. No modifications are required for a Relaying Party to support the presented protocol.

3.4.3.6 Deregistration

The third use case is the deregistration, which removes an existing OpenID identifier from the Provider. The presented protocol requires that the key or data of the user are stored on both sides. The client side possesses the private part of the Signing Key. The Provider stores the public part of the Signing Key and the associated UUID. Therefore, the deregistration can be realized with three possibilities:

- The user uses a function in the browser add-on to erase the private part of the Signing Key from the platform. Without this key, the authentication is not feasible anymore. This option is only reasonable if the Signing Key was used for exactly one OpenID identifier. Otherwise, the deletion of the key would also deregister the other OpenID identifiers related to the Signing Key. This approach is not optimal, because the public part of the Signing Key remains in the Provider as stale data and the identifier is still reserved for the user. The Provider can implement an additional functionality, which removes unused accounts after a certain period of time. This functionality, however, increases the effort for the management and also the final deregistration of an identifier is performed after a delay.

- Another option is that only the Provider performs the deregistration. In this case, the Provider sets up a form which allows a user to deregister his OpenID identifier. When a user requests the deregistration, the Provider removes the stored data associated to the user. This deletes also the related OpenID identifier instantly, although the private part of the Signing Key remains on the client side. This approach is appropriate when a Signing Key is used for multiple OpenID identifiers. The user can delete the Signing Key when he or she has assured that all identifiers related to the Signing Key were removed.

- The third option is the combination of the previous options. In this case, the add-on provides a functionality, which deletes the private part of the Signing Key simultaneously with the removal of the user data in the Provider. This procedure instantly removes the data on both sides without leaving stale data. To achieve this, a method has to be implemented, which triggers the deregistration on both sides. This approach is optimal, if one Signing Key is associated with one OpenID identifier.

One of these three methods can be chosen to accomplish the deregistration. The choice depends on effort, usability and security within the general conditions of the system.

3.4.3.7 Evaluation

The protocol enhances the security of the authentication, but also has some drawbacks. In comparison to a conventional authentication with a password, the presented concept is more complex, because of the signature. The signing operation is performed within the TPM, which has limited resources. This can lead to a remarkable delay in the authentication process.

Furthermore, the binding of the authentication to the TPM restricts the user to one platform. The user can authenticate only from the platform, which is equipped with the TPM that protects the Signing Key. This problem can be solved by registering multiple Signing Keys at the Provider. The user may use one Signing Key for each platform. In this case, a procedure for the registration of multiple platforms is required. Usually a user should use a platform, which is already registered, to submit Signing Keys of other platforms to the Provider. This approach is quite cumbersome, because the user needs to transfer the public part of the Signing Key to the registered platform. One possibility to solve this problem is the already mentioned dual approach, which allows the alternative login with password or with the Signing Key. This approach, however, has also security drawbacks.

3.4. DEVELOPED CONCEPTS

One advantage of the presented protocol is the secure authentication with a challenge-response protocol using a signature. It prevents phishing attacks, because the password is not transmitted to the Provider. An attacker would gain no advantage in the eavesdropping of the transmitted values. The Signing Key is protected by the TPM, which ensures that the key can only be used on the specific platform. The key is not migratable and cannot be transferred to another platform. Furthermore, the session management of the OpenID session and the TSS session offers an enhancement for the security and the usability. The timeout of the OpenID session can be reduced to increase the frequency of the authentication with the Provider. A higher frequency offers a higher security for the Relaying Party and if the TSS session remains active, the authentication does not require a user input. A compromise between security and usability has to be found within the general conditions of the application.

3.4.3.8 Summary

The presented concept describes a user authentication using the TPM within the OpenID system. The conventional password authentication to the Provider is replaced with a Signing Key, which is protected by the TPM. The platform of the user has to be equipped with a TPM and an add-on has to be installed in the User Agent. The user is verified locally on the platform using the TPM. The security in this authentication depends on the protection of the Signing Key, because it is the secret, which is verified by the Provider. The password to load the Signing Key has to be chosen carefully and needs to remain confidential. The protocol is efficient, because it requires only once the services of the PrivacyCA during the registration of the user. The enhanced protocol remains compatible to the existing OpenID specification, which eases the acceptance and the distribution of the concept.

3.4.4 Summary of the concepts

Several methods for the protection of content relevant for security were presented. The Trusted Computing technology was used and integrated into XML-based standards for the management and exchange of content. This enables an interoperable exchange and processing of the protected content.

Chapter 4

Implementation

The presented concepts were implemented in a prototype to verify the realizability and the functionalities. The separate concepts were aligned to each other and combined to a working Content Management System. The resulting implementation is an elaborated solution based on MPEG-21 and Trusted Computing technologies. The system works decentralized and requires only a possibility for the verification of the AIK keys, which can be either realized with a PrivacyCA or the DAA. As there are no mature implementations of the DAA, the PrivacyCA is applied in the prototype. The next sections introduce the use cases, the implementation and the description of the software components.

4.1 Application scenarios

The implemented software can be used in many application scenarios, where content management is involved and content is exchanged with security mechanisms. The implementation can be used for the management of unprotected content as well as the secure exchange of content relevant to security. This is achieved with different levels of security.

Unprotected content is managed and distributed with the descriptive metadata of the MPEG-A Open Access Application Format. The standard improves the sharing and indexing of free distributable content using the metadata based on MPEG-21 and MPEG-7. This metadata is used in the

4.2. ARCHITECTURE

implemented software components to identify the content and to provide the user a convenient interface for the management and sharing of the content.

An intermediate level of security is provided by the signatures, which can be applied to single Items or to all Items in a file. The signatures protect the authenticity and the integrity of the content, but they do not ensure the confidentiality. The signatures can be used for example to ensure that the content cannot be modified during the distribution.

The highest level of security is provided with the encryption of confidential content using the TPM technology. The aim is to secure the exchange of content in scenarios where it is in the user's best interest to have the content protected. One example are Enterprise Rights Management Systems, which manage and protect internal content from a company or organization. The system can also span multiple companies to allow an exchange of content from one company to another. The TPM is often embedded by default in business computers and laptops, which eases the support for the security features of the implementation. Another application domain of the software is the medical sector to protect the exchange of medical records. A digital exchange of data between physicians and patients would increase the efficiency in diagnosis and treatment. The security of the medical data is a central aspect, because the privacy of the patient has to be ensured. The MPEG-21 standards provide an optimal basis for the interoperable exchange of the medical data between heterogeneous platforms. The TPM is also a favorable security chip adequate for the wide application in this sector.

4.2 Architecture

The implementation consists of several components, which can be categorized in network services and client applications. Figure 4.1 shows an overview of the components and their interaction between each other.

It also shows the interaction of the components in the implementation. The TPM in the client is depicted at the bottom of the figure. It contains and protects the private keys of each user. Although not depicted, the keys can also be exported on an external storage device using Storage Keys. Each user has two private keys, which are for the two operations: signing and encrypting. The keys are generated within the TPM and are not migratable.

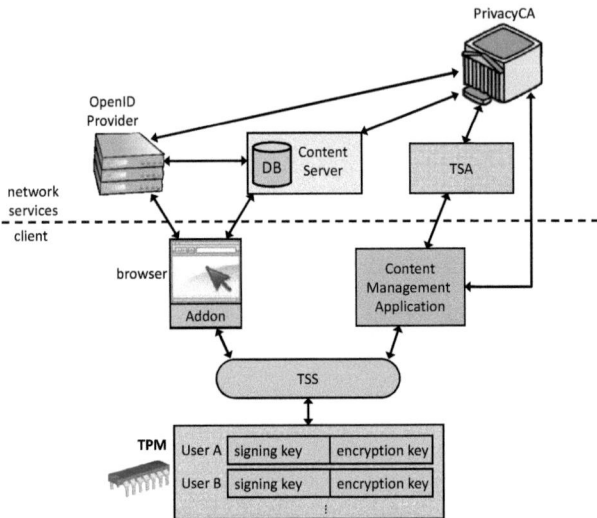

Figure 4.1: Overview of the system components

Above the TPM is an implementation of the TSS, which provides a high-level interface of the TPM functions for the applications. Two applications were developed for the client side, which use the functions of the TPM.

One application is the Content Management Application, which is the central application for the consumption and creation of content. It implements the complete file format and allows the management of the embedded metadata in the Items. For the creation and release of content, it uses the TSA to obtain a time reference value for secure timestamps. After the exchange of this reference value, the Content Management Application can issue secure timestamps offline without further communication with the TSA.

The other client application is the web browser with the integrated add-on. The browser performs the user authentication with an OpenID Provider using the TPM. The Relaying Party in this authentication is the Content Server, which is a web service providing and managing content in the system. The server allows users to comfortably search and browse content stored in

4.3. COMPONENTS

an internal database. The access control of the content is performed using OpenID and the REL in the metadata of the Item. This allows the Content Server to distribute the content to the appropriate users. If the user is authorized, he can download the content and use the Content Management Application to view and consume the content.

Most components were developed in the Java programming language [33], which is an object-oriented language designed to compile and execute the same source code on several platforms. This enables the execution of the implemented components on all platforms supported by Java. The full functionality is, however, only provided in the Linux operating system and its derivate, because some required components are not available for other operating systems.

4.3 Components

This section presents the implemented components and their interactions to each other in the system. At first the local components on the client are explained, which can be used for the creation and the consumption of content. After that, the components for the distribution and the exchange of content are described.

4.3.1 TPM Module and TSS

The choice of the TPM and TSS implementation is a challenging task. The existing TPMs in the market were evaluated in [93] with the result that the modules are partly incompatible to each other or do not implement all features of the specification. This creates difficulties in the realization and the interoperability between several platforms. Similar problems arise with TSS implementations, which are not interoperable with all TPMs. Furthermore, they are also incompatible with the applications, because some functions were implemented differently. As the TSS specification is also extensive, most TSS implementations are not elaborated and do not support all features.

One TSS implementation, which supports most of the TPM functions, is the TCG Software Stack for the Java Platform (jTSS) [28]. The software supports a set of TPMs and is available for different operating systems. One

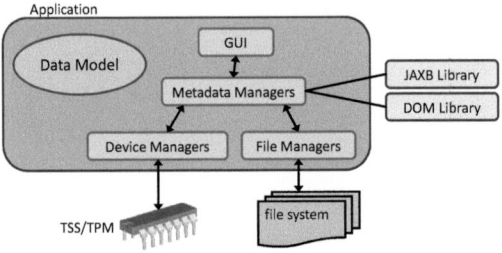

Figure 4.2: Architecture of the Content Management Application

of the supported devices is the TPM-Emulator [27], which emulates a TPM in software. An emulated TPM has the advantage that the implementing software can be exchanged and updated frequently. The implementation is also independent of faulty hardware implementations or incompatibilities between the manufacturers. For these reasons the presented prototype and its components use the combination of jTSS and TPM-Emulator. Hardware TPMs may work directly or with minor modifications, but they were not tested for full compatibility.

4.3.2 Content Management Application

The Content Management Application supports the creation and the consumption of files conform to the specification presented in section 2.4.2.1. The software implements the mentioned MPEG-21 and MPEG-7 standards and provides a convenient user interface to demonstrate the advantages of the format. The Java Programming language was used for the implementation. It can be used either as a file editor for the creation of conform files or as a viewer to consume created files.

4.3.2.1 Architecture

The architecture and internal structure of the application is depicted in figure 4.2.

The figure shows the application with its libraries and the interfaces to

4.3. COMPONENTS

the operating system. Internally the application can be categorized into the Data Model and the Managers. Both represent several classes and interfaces. The Data Model is depicted in green and it stores all information during the execution of the program. The stored information is either related to the content or to the user management. The data related to the content represents the resource and the metadata within an Item. The metadata is the XML-based descriptive information about the content and its license. Within the software the metadata remains in a derived from of the XML format to ease the parsing and saving of the metadata.

The data related to the user management contains information about the users and their cryptographic keys. The user information includes, for example, an identifier, the user name or an address. This information can be embedded during the creation of a file and allows for the recognition of the user who created the file. The cryptographic keys are required for the signing and encryption of the content. They are mainly references to keys stored in the TPM, which can be applied or retrieved from the TPM. The retrieval of a key is required for the encryption of content.

The Data Model is used by the Managers, which consist of the Graphical User Interface (GUI), the Metadata Managers, the Device Managers and the File Managers. The GUI creates a user interface and interacts with the user. It allows the user to create new files or to consume existing files. All metadata elements from MPEG-21 and MPEG-7 are supported and presented to the user. During the creation of a file, the user can modify the metadata by changing the information in the respective fields.

These modifications are passed to the Metadata Managers, which validate and save the information in the Data Model. These Managers create, parse and validate the XML metadata from the MPEG-21 and MPEG-7 standards. For the XML processing, they use the JAXB- and DOM library for the importing and exporting of information to the Data Model. Furthermore, they verify signatures and perform the de- or encryption of the content. When a file is finalized and saved to the file system, the Metadata Managers call the respective methods of the File Managers. The File Managers are also involved when an existing file is opened and consumed. They implement the file format and enable the creation and the parsing of files conform to the specified file format.

The keys for the signature and encryption are stored and loaded using

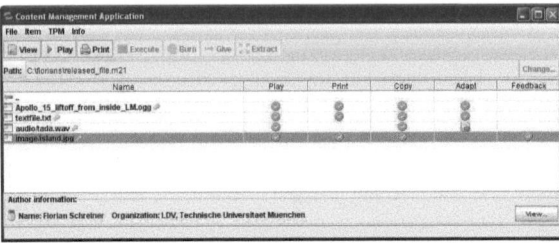

Figure 4.3: Main window of the Content Management Application

the Device Managers, which provide an interface to a cryptographic device. The implemented software supports the TPM as principal device for the key storage. The Managers connect to the TSS of the operating system and create the required sessions to send commands to the TPM. Besides the support for the TPM, a software device is implemented, which emulates the interface of the Device Manager in a plain software implementation. This allows the usage of the software in environments where no TPM is available, but lacks the respective security enhancements of a real TPM. The software device can be used in particular for testing or development purposes. The abstracted interface of the Device Managers additionally eases the support for other devices like smart cards.

4.3.2.2 Functionalities

The software supports two modes of operation: the creation mode and the consumption mode. In the creation mode, the user can create files, which are conform to the specification. The user inserts resources as Items into the file and adds metadata to the Items. When the user has finished the compilation of the file, he or she can finalize it and save it to the file system. During this finalization, the signatures are created and the content is encrypted if selected. The created file is a package, which cannot be modified anymore. The user can open this file again and the application switches in the consumption mode. In this mode, the user can view the Items in the file with their attached metadata. He or she can request the access to the resource, which is transparently decrypted if required and presented to the user.

4.3. COMPONENTS

To get an impression of the application, the main window of the application in the consumption mode is shown in figure 4.3 as an example. In this state, the application displays a table, which contains the Items of a file with their respective license properties. The toolbar on the top of the window offers several functions for consumption to the user. The user can for example view an Item, which presents the embedded metadata like the author or the license of the content. The aim of the software is not to restrict the user, but to notify him if he intends to perform an action, which might not be allowed for some content. It is in the interest and the responsibility of the user to respect the license conditions to avoid legal conflicts. These can be also seen in the further functionalities of the implementation, which are mentioned shortly:

- **License pattern:** The user can predefine licenses, which he intends to use frequently. These licenses can be applied in a single step to the content. It sets the defined copyright information and associates the rights expressions with the content.

- **Relationships between Items:** The software allows to specify a relationship, which defines that one Item is an adaptation of another Item. The relationship may be set in both directions declaring that the Item is an adaptation of another Item, or the Item was adapted to another Item. The software also interprets the REL to notify the user if the right for adaptation is granted.

- **Copying of Items:** This feature allows the user to copy an Item to another file, while the attached metadata and signatures remain intact. This copy enables the aggregation or combination of different content into a new file. This function also uses the REL to guide the user in the copy procedure. The software displays which Item grants the right to copy to the user. Furthermore, he is notified whether the right to copy the Item is granted in the REL of the source.

- **License Acknowledgment:** In the consumption mode, the user has to acknowledge the license and its conditions before he can use the content. This ensures that the user is aware of the license and that he or she knows what he or she is allowed to do with the content.

- **Rendering Engines:** For the consumption of the content, a rendering engine is required, which understands the format of the content and can display it. The software supports the extraction out of the content to the file system, which is applicable to all content types. The content is saved as a file and can be opened with a separate program, which can display the content. Besides the extraction, a couple of rendering engines are also integrated into the implementation. These rendering engines are able to display images, audio (wave format), video (theora codec) and plain text directly from the file.

4.3.2.3 Cryptographic operations

The cryptographic operations like encryption and signatures are implemented with a combination of libraries and TPM commands. The libraries are used for operations, which cannot be executed in the TPM, e.g., the symmetric encryption of content. The libraries are integrated according to the Java Cryptography Architecture (JCA) [14], which is part of the Java Platform Standard Edition (Java SE). The available cryptographic functions are additionally extended with the Bouncy Castle Crypto APIs [7] which provides support for X.509 certificates and qualified timestamps.

The connection to the TPM uses the jTSS as an intermediate layer between the TPM and the application. The application connects to the jTSS and establishes a context, which can be understood as a session for the connection. Within this context, the application can trigger the creation of AIKs for the verification of internal keys of the TPM. This includes the execution of the protocol with the PrivacyCA to obtain the AIK credentials. They enable another party to verify the corresponding AIK. Both the AIKs and their credentials are stored as files on the file system. An AIK can be loaded into the TPM to certify keys protected by the TPM. Furthermore, the files can then be exchanged with other parties which allows them to verify the signatures created by the AIK.

The encryption of content is performed as described in section 3.4.1.3 using the JCA. After the transmission, the Content Management Application passes the encrypted content key to the jTSS. The TPM decrypts the key and the application can decrypt the content.

The creation of the signature is more complex, because the standard

4.3. COMPONENTS

implementation for the creation of XML signatures has to be adapted to integrate the TPM in the creation process. The standard implementation uses the private key directly to sign the hash value of the document. This method cannot be reused, because the TPM protects the private key that only the TPM can perform the signing operation. To perform this function, a new method for the creation of a signature was implemented and integrated into the standard signing operation. This provides the opportunity to reuse most of the standard implementation for the XML processing and only involves the TPM for the signing operation. This also increases the compatibility with existing applications, because only minimal modifications are required to integrate the TPM in the creation of a signature. The modifications deal with different parameters to address the content of the TPM and to reference a specific key in the TPM. The created signature is validated as other signatures, because the TPM is not required in the verification. The public key is verified using the signature created with the AIK key and the credentials issued from the PrivacyCA.

4.3.2.4 Timestamps

The implementation also offers the possibility to enhance the signature with a qualified timestamp as specified in section 3.4.2. The timestamps can be created on the basis of the tick counters of the TPM. They can be optionally added to the signature to allow an author to decide whether a timestamp is required. The implementation uses an external TSA to obtain a verifiable time basis and connects this time basis to a tick counter of the TPM. After that, the TPM can issue qualified timestamps, which are integrated into the created signatures conform to the XMLDSig standard.

Internally the implementation contains classes for the representation of the exchanged values. The TSA is realized with functions from the Bouncy Castle Crypto API, which works as a network service to issue qualified timestamps. The network service is based on the TCP/IP protocol and supports a communication using the HTTP protocol.

The Content Management Application is the intermediate party between the TSA and the TPM and manages the creation of the timestamps using the TPM. The creation of these timestamps can be divided in four steps:

- AIK creation,

- binding of the tick counter to a timestamp,
- timestamp creation and
- validation.

The created values after each step are temporarily saved to the file system, which enables the independent execution of the steps. The saving of the values allows their future use independent of the intermediate states of the application or the operating system. For example, the application may be closed at any time or even the operating system may be shut down as long as the tick counter remains intact.

AIK creation The first step is the creation of an AIK, which is a prerequisite, because it is required for the verification of the values from the tick counter. These values are signed by an AIK, which is in turn verifiable with the AIK credentials. Both allow a recipient to verify the authenticity if the tick value originates from an authentic TPM. After the creation of the AIK, the execution of the following steps can be triggered.

Binding a tick counter to a timestamp In this step the absolute timestamp from the TSA is connected with two tickstamps from the TPM. At first, the implementation requests the first tickstamp from the TPM and transmits its hash value to the TSA. The communication to the TSA is realized with the Time-Stamp Protocol (TSP) standard, which is the protocol prevalently used for this task. The TSA is identified with a string, which is given by the user. It contains the information, which protocol has to be used and how the connection to the TSA can be established. At the end of the communication, the TSA returns a qualified timestamp to the application. The application hashes the first tickstamp and transmits this value to the TPM to create the second tickstamp. After that, all stamps and the AIK used for the tickstamps are stored in the file system. From that point on, the TPM can be used to create qualified timestamps for every content that will be published. This can be performed as long as the session of the tick counter remains intact.

Timestamp creation The timestamp is created as a part of the signature process at the time, when a content is lastly signed before its publication.

4.3. COMPONENTS

At first the data stored in the file system is loaded into the application. Furthermore, the document to sign is hashed and the hash value is sent to the TPM. From this hash value the TPM creates the third tickstamp using the previously initialized tick counter. Finally, the three tickstamps, the timestamp, and the AIK are stored in a XML document and integrated into the signature of the document based on the XMLDSig standard.

Validation The recipient of a signature has to validate the timestamp and the set of tickstamps to verify their correctness. The Content Management Application also contains an implementation of this validation. Within the application, the validation is performed when a file with several Items is opened. At first the TPM-based timestamp is extracted from the XML signature and the TSA-timestamp and the tickstamps are extracted from the XML document. These values are then verified in the following steps:

- In the first step, the AIK is verified using the credentials issued by the PrivacyCA. The client has to trust the PrivacyCA either directly or using a certificate chain in a Public Key Infrastructure.

- Then, the tickstamps with their values are verified using the public part of the AIK. The hash of the values in the tickstamp is recalculated and compared to the value in the signature.

- In the next step, a recalculation of the hash values given in the tickstamps is performed. For each tickstamp the corresponding document is hashed and the resulting value is compared to the value stored in the tickstamp.

- To complete the verification of the tickstamps, the consistency of the nonces has to verified. The nonces of all tickstamps in a timestamp have to be identical to ensure that they originate from the same tick counter of a specific TPM. It also ensures that the tick counter was not reset during the creation of the timestamp.

- Then, the time interval between the first two tickstamps is calculated. This time interval reflects the imprecision of the timestamp to the absolute time value of the TSA-timestamp. The imprecision has to be below a certain threshold to ensure that the time is within appropriate boundaries.

- Finally the signature of the TSA-timestamp is verified using the certificate of the TSA. Similar to the PrivacyCA, the TSA and their timestamps have to be trusted.

The order of these steps is not important. If the verification in all steps was successful, the TPM-based timestamp is valid. The point in time, in which the document was signed, can be obtained with the TSA-timestamp and the time difference between the second and third tickstamp. The tick values of these tickstamps is converted to a time value, which is added to the absolute time value of the TSA-timestamp. The imprecision of the resulting time is given in the time difference between the first and second tickstamp. They define the lower and upper boundary, which has to remain below a certain threshold. The threshold can be defined depending on the particular application scenario. In the developed implementation using the TPM emulator and the presented TSA, the imprecision is about one second. Thus a threshold of several seconds should be sufficient under these conditions. In the case when a real TPM is used, the threshold depends mainly on the performance of the respective TPM.

4.3.3 Content Server

The Content Server is a web service, which works as an intermediate party between the author and the consumer to enhance the distribution. The server has an integrated repository of Items, which contains and indexes the content with its attached metadata. A user can connect to the server with a browser to view the content in the repository. He or she can download content from the server and consume it locally.

The Content Server is implemented in the Java programming language as a Java Servlet [15], which is executed in a servlet container. As servlet container, the Apache Tomcat [3] is applied. The implemented web application uses AJAX technology [2] to create an interactive user interface with asynchronous loading of the data from the server to the client.

4.3.3.1 Metadata

The server makes use of the metadata within the Items. The server parses all Items in the database and indexes the Items in several categories. The cre-

4.3. COMPONENTS

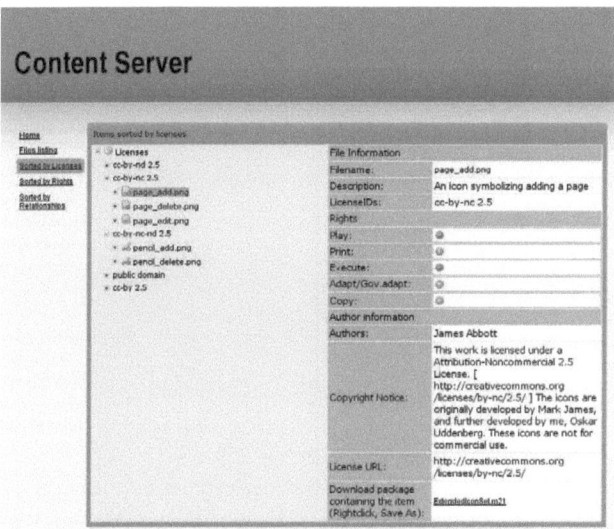

Figure 4.4: User interface of the Content Server in a browser

ated indexes are presented to the user in a tree structure using the JavaScript programming language [8]. This structure enables the user to comfortably browse and search the database for content which matches certain criteria. The implemented categories are the type of license, the rights expressions, and the relationships between derived Items. A screenshot of the interface with the category license type is shown in figure 4.4.

In this example, the tree structure contains the different license types of the Items in the database. Within each license type, the server shows all Items which are published with that license. In this example the Items are icons, which are displayed on the left side of each entry in the tree structure. The user can select an Item and the metadata of the Item is shown in a table on the right side. The presented metadata assists the user in the browsing and searching of Items. The user has a clear overview of the most important properties of the Item, which also eases the comparison of several Items between each other. This view also offers the user the possibility to download the Item in the specified MPEG-21 file format. The downloaded file can then be consumed on the local platform.

The Content Server works as a mediator and can thus distribute files to the correct users. Each user can only see the files, which are authorized for him or her. This authorization depends on the REL license, which is part of each Item. The authorization requires an authentication mechanism, which verifies the user currently connected to the server. Such an authentication mechanism is shown in the next section.

4.3.3.2 User Authentication

The Content Sever uses the OpenID system to authenticate users for the distribution of the content. According to the OpenID specification, the Content Server acts like the Relaying Party, which trusts the authentication from the OpenID Provider. The method for authentication relies in the responsibility of the user and the Relaying Party. The user has to decide which Provider offers a method for authentication trustworthy enough for the exchanged content. The Relaying Party also has to know which Provider offers a sufficient security level.

The OpenID system is supported in the Content Server by a login form, which the user can use to enter his OpenID Identifier. After the user has entered and submitted his identifier, the form executes the OpenID authentication mechanism conform to the specification. This includes the discovery and redirection mechanism to the OpenID Provider.

The user performs the authentication with the Provider, which can be accomplished with a password or the TPM authentication as presented in this book. The implementation of the authentication with the TPM is shown in section 4.3.4. After the authentication, the User Agent is the redirected back to a page of the Content Server. This page verifies the response from the Provider. If the verification was successful, the Content Server creates a user session to automatically identify the user during the communication. The session is managed with a cookie, which contains a nonce as identifier of the session. The server stores this value together with the OpenID identifier in the database. This enables the server to re-identify the requests of the user. If a user without such a cookie or an invalid session tries to connect directly to a governed content, the user is redirected to the login screen for authentication.

Furthermore, the implementation provides a logout functionality. This function is available when a session was successfully established. It allows the user to invalidate the active session with the Content Server. It deletes the cookie from the browser and the Content Server removes the session from the database.

4.3.3.3 Key management

Besides the user authentication, the server also includes a key repository, which stores the encryption keys for each user. These keys are the public parts of asymmetric encryption keys, which can be used to transfer content in encrypted form to the user. Each user can upload an encryption key, which is assigned to his account. This key is used in the Content Server for the encrypted transfer of the content to the client.

The server provides a separate page, which enables the user to view, upload, and delete these encryption keys. The user can obtain a key from the Content Management Application, which uses the TPM to create and store the private part of the key. The public part of the key is exported out of the TPM and stored in a XML-file using the XMLDSig standard. The user then uploads the key to the Content Server to enable the encrypted transfer of content.

Another functionality of the server is the uploading of content. The user can create MPEG-21 files with Items using the Management Application and upload these files to the server. To upload a file, the user loads a specific page from the server and then transmits the files to the server. This file can also be encrypted using a public key of the server to ensure the confidentiality. Upon reception, the server validates the file, stores it in the repository and releases it.

4.3.4 Browser add-on

The browser add-on is developed for the Mozilla Firefox internet browser [18], which supports the development of add-ons to extend the functionalities of the browser. The developed add-on augments the browser with the support for the authentication protocol using a signing key stored in the TPM. It communicates with the TPM and performs the local operation for the

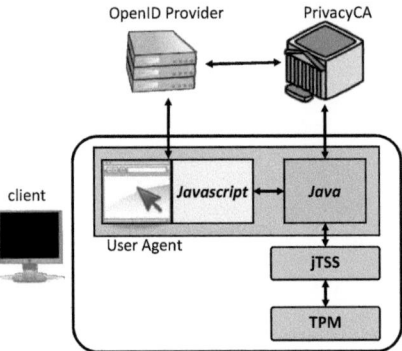

Figure 4.5: Architecture of the browser add-on and its connections

authentication to the Provider. The add-on consists of several components, which are presented in the next section. In the section after, the implemented functionalities are described.

4.3.4.1 Architecture

The architecture of the browser add-on and the connections to external components are shown in figure 4.5.

Within the client there are the User Agent, the jTSS and the TPM. The User Agent is the Firefox browser, which consists of two parts: the browser with a JavaScript add-on and a Java implementation. The add-on is implemented in JavaScript, because it is the default language for the Firefox browser. The browser provides a documented interface for the creation of add-ons to extend the functionality of the browser. The developed implemantation behaves like a normal add-on for the browser, which can be installed with the usual procedure. After this installation, some additional rights have to be assigned to the add-on, which are required for the communication with the TPM. When the add-on is successfully installed, it extends the user interface and interacts with the user using additional entries in the context menu and dialogs. The added entries in the context menu are required to trigger functions for the authentication procedure. An example for

4.3. COMPONENTS

such an operation is the creation of a signing key. When the user triggers such a function, the add-on forwards the request to the Java implementation to execute the operation. The JavaScript implementation works thus as a mediator between the browser and the Java implementation.

The Java implementation is the central component, which establishes a connection to the jTSS or the PrivacyCA as required. It provides a high-level API to the JavaScript implementation to execute the functions the user triggers. It implements the logic behind these functions to centrally manage the execution and error processing. The Java implementation can connect to the jTSS and manages the sessions with the TPM. It uses the jTSS to create, register or load the signing keys. Furthermore, it implements functions to use such a signing key for the creation of signatures on data provided by the JavaScript implementation. Another signature can be created over the signing key using the AIK, which is required to verify the signing key. Moreover, the Java implementation can connect to the PrivacyCA to create the credentials for the AIK.

The Java implementation is not essentially required in the prototype, because the logic could have been also implemented in JavaScript. In this ideal case the JavaScript implementation could interact directly with the jTSS. The Java implementation was added to ease the development and to prevent possible side effects and additional efforts, which can occur when the JavaScript implementation connects directly to the complex API of the jTSS. In a productive implementation, the Java implementation can be rewritten in JavaScript and integrated into the add-on.

4.3.4.2 Functionalities

This section presents the functionalities of the added User Interface in the browser and the implementation of the authentication procedure with the OpenID Provider.

Ownership The ownership has to be taken in the TPM to enable the creation of signing keys for an authentication. Furthermore, the implementation also allows to undo this operation and to clear the ownership of the TPM.

This operation is implemented as specified by the TCG. The user can perform this operation directly and conveniently in the browser and is not dependent on another application. As the operation is used as standardized, it is not essentially required to be performed by the browser add-on. An already existing ownership can be reused or the operation can be also executed from another application.

Session management The communication with the jTSS is bound to sessions, which are established between the TPM and the application. They are required to create and use signature keys for signing operations. The Java implementation creates these sessions and manages them. For the establishment of a session, the user has to provide the owner secret to access the TPM. Every user using the TPM for the authentication has to know this secret. Thus on a single-user platform, this secret can be only known to the owner of the platform. If multiple users are using the platform, the secret can be empty or shared with all users. After the establishment of a session, the user can load signing keys into the TPM. A loaded signing key can be used multiple times within a session for the authentication at a Provider. This increases the efficiency and follows the principle of a single sign on system. It is valid under the assumption that one instance of the browser is only used by a single user.

To terminate this session, the user can use the logout function of the browser add-on. This function unloads the signing key from the TPM and terminates the session. This is also automatically performed, when the browser application is closed to prevent that another user can reuse an existing session.

Creation of signing keys After the ownership is taken and a session is established, the user can create a new signing key in the TPM. The new key is non-migratable and can be used to create signatures for the authentication with the OpenID Provider. Together with the generation of the key in the TPM, an AIK is created, which is used to sign the signing key. Furthermore, the AIK credentials are requested from the PrivacyCA, which allow a third party to verify the keys. The public part of the AIK and its credentials are then stored as a file onto the file system. This file can then be used for the registration at an OpenID Provider. The private part of the key is also stored on the file system encrypted with a Storage Key using the persistent storage functionality of the jTSS.

4.3. COMPONENTS

The implementation can differentiate multiple signing keys with their UUID identifier used in the TPM. This identifier is also transmitted to the Provider during the registration of the user. When the user registers at a Provider, the Provider associates the public part of the signing key and the identifier to the user. The identifier is retransmitted to the user when the authentication is performed. This enables the implementation to load the corresponding key into the TPM for the creation of the signature.

Authentication procedure The authentication is initiated, when the browser add-on recognizes a Provider, which supports the presented protocol. A Provider supporting the protocol sets a specific cookie with a defined and unique identifier, which the browser add-on can recognize. The recognition is achieved by monitoring the exchanged HTML data of the browser. The Firefox browser offers a listener mechanism that enables an add-on to be notified on certain events in the browser. One of these listener methods also offers a notification, when a cookie is set in the browser. This notification method is used in the add-on to check if the specific cookie from an OpenID Provider is set.

If this is the case, the browser add-on triggers the execution of the protocol and establishes a session to the jTSS. Within this cookie, the Provider transmits a nonce, which is used for the challenge-response authentication. Furthermore, it contains the UUID of the signing key, which is used for the signature. The add-on checks if the requested key is already loaded into the TPM. This is the case, if the key was already loaded in a preceding execution of the authentication protocol. If the key is not yet loaded, the signing key belonging to the transmitted UUID is looked up and loaded into the TPM. Then, the nonce is sent to the TPM, which signs it using the signing key. After that, the resulting signature is transmitted to the Provider via HTML using the post command. The answer to this command redirects the browser to a specific URL within the site of the Provider. The Provider uses this URL to notify the user about the result of the authentication. If the authentication was successful, the user is automatically redirected back to the Relaying Party as authenticated user. If the authentication failed, the Provider displays an error message and offers the user to retry the authentication.

The established session with the TPM, which was created to gain access to the signing key, is not automatically terminated after an authentication. The session is kept open to allow another authentication without creating a new session. The current state of the session is signaled to the user with an icon in the status bar. The logout function in the implementation terminates such a session with the TPM, which unloads the signing key from the TPM. To reload the key, the user has to start a new session and load the key again in the TPM.

4.3.5 OpenID Provider

The OpenID Provider is implemented as a web server using Java Server Pages (JSP). The software is based on the openid4java implementation [24], which is a Java implementation of an OpenID Provider conform to the OpenID 2.0 specification. This implementation is extended with the presented authentication protocol. The developed Provider can be used for the authentication with any Relaying Party supporting OpenID. It depends on the support of the browser whether the extended authentication involving the TPM can be applied.

The OpenID Provider supports three functionalities: the authentication, the registration, and the deregistration. These functionalities are explained in the following subsections.

4.3.5.1 Registration

The OpenID Provider works as a user database, which saves the data of all users and assigns an OpenID Identifier to each user. The registration is the functionality, which allows a user to add his identity to this database and to obtain an identifier. The information the user has to provide during the registration, e.g., an e-mail address or phone number, is application specific and not examined further in this book.

For the application of the presented protocol, the user has to submit the public part of the signing key and its credentials during the registration. This enables the Provider to assign the key to the user, which is required for the authentication. The openid4java implementation provides a registration form, which creates a new user in the database and assigns an identifier to the user. This registration was extended with additional fields to upload the

4.3. COMPONENTS

signing key, its UUID and its credentials. After the upload, the implementation verifies the signing key using the AIK and its credentials to ensure that the key originates from a TPM and is protected by it. The UUID of the key is required for the authentication. It notifies the browser add-on of the identifier of the signing key in the persistent storage of the TPM. If this validation is successful, the user information and the keys are stored in the database. The Provider shows the user a page that the authentication was successful and displays the created OpenID identifier.

After the registration the user can use the Provider to authenticate to a Relaying Party.

4.3.5.2 Authentication

When the user wants to log in to a Relaying Party, the Relaying Party redirects the User Agent to a specific JSP page of the Provider. The Provider first checks if the required parameters for the authentication are present and valid. If the parameters are not valid, the user is redirected to a page, which shows an error message. The parameters are the usual parameters according to the OpenID specification. The Provider checks in the database if the user is registered and loads the data. If the data contains the signing key, the Provider knows that the user can perform the extended authentication with the TPM. In this case, the Provider creates a cookie, which is assigned to the browser session of the user. In this cookie, the Provider puts a nonce value and the UUID of the signing key in the TPM of the user.

The cookie is then sent back to the User Agent in the response. The cookie has a specific identifier, which allows the add-on in the browser to recognize the cookie and to trigger the signing procedure. It uses the UUID in the cookie to load the respective key from the persistent storage into the TPM. After that, it signs the nonce value with the signing key in the TPM. The browser add-on retransmits the signature back to the Provider as a variable within a HTML post command using a specific identifier.

The Provider recognizes the signed nonce and performs the validation of the signature. It loads the public part of the signing key from the database, decrypts the signed nonce, and compares the result to the nonce previously sent to the user. If the values are equal, the user is authenticated. The implementation also contains some error processing for the cases that an error occurs. One example is that the browser add-on cannot load the signing key, because the user cannot provide the corresponding secret. In this case, the add-on sets a constant value as signed nonce. The Provider recognizes this value and displays a corresponding error message.

After the authentication, the Provider sets an internal variable to indicate the success of the authentication. Then, the Provider builds the redirect back to the originating Relaying Party according to the OpenID specification. The Relaying Party recognizes the successful authentication and the user is logged in.

4.3.5.3 Deregistration

The deregistration removes a user from the database and deletes the assigned data of the user. Only the user who created the account, can deregister himself. A user has to authenticate himself to the Provider to request the removal. To remove an account, the user can load a page for this purpose from the Provider. This page allows the user to log into the site in the same way as to a Relaying Party. The authentication is thus performed with the Provider as the Relaying Party. The authentication is then performed equally to the normal procedure. If the authentication was successful, the Provider deletes all information of the user from the database.

4.4 Summary

The presented implementation realizes a solution for the management and protection of content based on MPEG-21 standards and Trusted Computing technology. The software implements the developed concepts, which are aligned to each other to realize an overall user and key management. The system works decentralized, because the users can exchange their data directly from user to user. To increase the convenience, a user may involve a Content Server for the distribution of the content. The Content Server as well as the OpenID Provider and the PrivacyCA can be operated multiple times by different parties. This offers the users the flexibility to choose a service, which fulfills required criteria like high reliability or trustworthiness. The implemented prototype shows the realizability of the developed concepts and demonstrates their functionalities.

Chapter 5

Conclusion

This book presents several improvements for content management systems based on the MPEG-21 standards. For free distributable content the interoperable sharing and collaboration was improved with a selected set of common metadata. This metadata enables the enhancement of the user experience in the consumption, reusing and indexing of specific content. The MPEG-21 standards provide a comprehensive set of tools, which are used as a basis for the selected metadata. The metadata describes the content, its license, and a feedback mechanism. The licenses defined by Creative Commons are investigated in detail as representatives for many other licenses in this domain. Several forms of representation and declaration of the license enhance the efficient processing of the license and the notification of the user. The feedback mechanism enriches the format with a mechanism to inform the author, which eases the management and enables the linking of content. The standardization of this metadata in the Open Access Application Format standard shows the importance and the potential impact to the sharing and collaboration of free distributable content.

Furthermore, the security for the storage and exchange of content is enhanced using the Trusted Computing technology within the MPEG-21 framework. A concept for the key management shows the feasibility of protecting confidential content in decentralized systems. The choice of an appropriate protection and exchange of the content relies in the responsibility of the user. The proposed concept does not require a specific method of transmission or modifications in the operating system and is therefore widely applicable. The concept presents an extension to the MPEG-21 framework and describes the integration of the required information in the metadata of the content.

Another improvement is the integration of qualified timestamps created by the TPM in digital signatures. These timestamps can be created by the TPM without a permanent connection to a trusted third party for a secure time basis. The specific timestamp data from the TPM is mapped to an optimal representation in XML, which is aligned to the most important standards for digital signatures in XML. It also shows methods for the integration of the developed representation within the standards to embed the timestamp directly within the signature.

The authentication of users within the OpenID system is improved by exploiting the TPM as a secure key storage device. The conventional password authentication is replaced by a challenge response authentication with signatures, which are created by the TPM. The password of the user is not transmitted anymore, which prevents the threat of a phishing attack. The security relies in the protection of the private part of the asymmetric key, which is bound to the TPM and cannot be read out of the device. It thus offers a higher level of security, because the key is only available on the specific platform, which is in possession of the authentic user. The presented protocol is compatible with the existing OpenID specification to foster the acceptance and adoption of the proposal.

In the last chapter an implementation is presented, which realizes all the described concepts and integrates them as components of a content management system. It is based on the MPEG-21 framework and uses the Trusted Computing technologies as a security basis for the protection of content. Users of the system can exchange their data decentralized directly from user to user. The OpenID system provides a global identity management and authentication mechanism, which enables the referencing of other users. The keys for the encryption and signatures are stored and protected in the TPM. The user decides and manages the keys, which enables the flexible and independent usage of multiple keys for several identities or different types of content.

Bibliography

[1] Adobe LiveCycle Rights Management ES2. Available online at http://www.adobe.com/products/livecycle/rightsmanagement/; visited on October 3rd 2010. Website [Online].

[2] Ajax: A New Approach to Web Applications. Available online at http://www.adaptivepath.com/ideas/essays/archives/000385.php; visited on April 4th 2010. Website [Online].

[3] Apache Tomcat. Available online at http://tomcat.apache.org; visited on February 23th 2010. Website [Online].

[4] Apple Fairplay - Thoughts on Music. Available online at http://www.apple.com/hotnews/thoughtsonmusic/; visited on October 3rd 2010. Website [Online].

[5] Axmedis - Automating Production of Cross Media Content for Multichannel Distribution. Available online at http://www.axmedis.org; visited on August 3rd 2010. Website [Online].

[6] Berlin Declaration on Open Access to Knowledge in the Sciences and Humanities. Available online at http://www.zim.mpg.de/openaccess-berlin/berlindeclaration.html; visited on January 30th 2010. Website [Online].

[7] Bouncy Castle Crypto APIs. Available online at http://www.bouncycastle.org/java.html; visited on Mai 19th 2010. Website [Online].

[8] Core JavaScript 1.5 Reference. Available online at https://developer.mozilla.org/en/docs/Core_JavaScript_1.5_Reference; visited on January 28th 2010. Website [Online].

[9] Creative Commons. Available online at http://creativecommons.org/; visited on January 28th 2010. Website [Online].

[10] DCMI Metadata Terms. Available online at http://dublincore.org/documents/dcmi-terms; visited on June 6th 2010. Website [Online].

[11] Digital Media Project (DMP). Available online at http://www.dmpf.org; visited on July 26th 2010. Website [Online].

[12] European Telecommunications Standards Institute (ETSI). Available online at http://www.etsi.org; visited on April 27th 2010. Website [Online].

[13] Interoperable Digital Rights Management Platform. Available online at http://open.dmpf.org//dmp1300.pdf; visited on July 26th 2010. Website [Online].

[14] Java Cryptography Architecture (JCA) Reference Guide. Available online at http://download.oracle.com/docs/cd/E17409_01/javase/6/docs/technotes/guides/security/crypto/CryptoSpec.html; visited on June 27th 2010. Website [Online].

[15] Java Servlet 3.0 Specification. Available online at http://jcp.org/aboutJava/communityprocess/final/jsr315/index.html; visited on February 23th 2010. Website [Online].

[16] Microsoft Windows Media - Verwaltung digitaler Rechte (DRM). Available online at http://www.microsoft.com/windows/windowsmedia/de/drm/default.aspx; visited on October 2nd 2010. Website [Online].

[17] Moving Picture Experts Group (MPEG). Available online at http://mpeg.chiariglione.org; visited on February 25th 2010. Website [Online].

[18] Mozilla Firefox. Available online at http://www.firefox.com/; visited on January 28th 2010. Website [Online].

[19] Mozilla Public License. Available online at http://www.mozilla.org/MPL/MPL-1.1.html; visited on February 22th 2010. Website [Online].

[20] Open Digital Rights Language (ODRL). Available online at http://odrl.net; visited on August 7th 2010. Website [Online].

BIBLIOGRAPHY 139

[21] Open Mobile Alliance (OMA). Available online at http://www.openmobilealliance.org; visited on August 8th 2010. Website [Online].

[22] Open Source Initiative. Available online at http://www.opensource.org; visited on April 23th 2010. Website [Online].

[23] OpenID 2009 Year in Review. Available online at http://openid.net/2009/12/16/openid-2009-year-in-review; visited on June 5th 2010. Website [Online].

[24] Openid4java - OpenID 2.0 Java Libraries. Available online at http://code.google.com/p/openid4java/; visited on March 7th 2010. Website [Online].

[25] Oracle Information Rights Management. Available online at http://www.oracle.com/us/products/middleware/content-management/information-rights-mgmt/index.html; visited on October 3rd 2010. Website [Online].

[26] SmartRM. Available online at http://www.smartrm.com; visited on August 6th 2010. Website [Online].

[27] Software-based TPM Emulator. Available online at http://tpm-emulator.berlios.de/index.html; visited on April 5th 2010. Website [Online].

[28] TCG Software Stack for the Java Platform. Available online at http://trustedjava.sourceforge.net/index.php?item=jtss/readme; visited on June 22th 2010. Website [Online].

[29] Trusted Computing Group. Available online at http://www.trustedcomputinggroup.org; visited on January 12th 2010. Website [Online].

[30] VeriSign's OpenID SeatBelt Plugin. Available online at https://pip.verisignlabs.com/seatbelt.do; visited on August 9th 2010. Website [Online].

[31] Wikimedia Commons. Available online at http://commons.wikimedia.org; visited on April 13th 2010. Website [Online].

[32] Wikimedia Commons: current statistics. Available online at http://commons.wikimedia.org/wiki/Special:Statistics; visited on April 19th 2010. Website [Online].

[33] Sun Microsystems, Inc., Java programming language. Available online at http://java.sun.com; visited on February 5th 2010., 1995. Website [Online].

[34] *XMP Specification*. Adobe Systems Incorporated, 2005. Available online at http://www.adobe.com/devnet/xmp/pdfs/xmp_specification.pdf; visited on August 7th 2010. Website [Online].

[35] Altova GmbH, XMLSpy 2007. Available online at http://www.altova.com/xmlspy.html; visited on April 27th 2010., 2007. Website [Online].

[36] H. Abelson, B. Adida, M. Linksvayer, and N. Yergler. *ccREL: The Creative Commons Rights Expression Language*. 2008. Available online at http://wiki.creativecommons.org/images/d/d6/Ccrel-1.0.pdf; visited on August 5th 2010. Website [Online].

[37] C. Adams, P. Cain, D. Pinkas, and R. Zuccherato. Internet X.509 Public Key Infrastructure - Time-Stamp Protocol (TSP). Technical Report RFC 3161, The Internet Engineering Task Force (IETF), 2001. http://www.ietf.org/rfc/rfc3161.txt.

[38] ANSI X9.95:2005. *Trusted Time Stamp Management and Security*. American National Standards Institute (ANSI), 2005.

[39] T. Berners-Lee, R. Fielding, and L. Masinter. Uniform Resource Identifier (URI): Generic Syntax. Technical Report RFC 3986, The Internet Engineering Task Force (IETF), 2005. http://www.ietf.org/rfc/rfc3986.txt.

[40] T. Berners-Lee, L. Masinter, and M. McCahill. Uniform Resource Locators (URL). Technical Report RFC 1738, The Internet Engineering Task Force (IETF), 1994. http://www.ietf.org/rfc/rfc1738.txt.

[41] T. Bray, J. Paoli, C. M. Sperberg-McQueen, E. Maler, and F. Yergeau. Extensible Markup Language (XML) 1.0 (Fifth Edition). Technical report, World Wide Web Consortium (W3C), 2008.

BIBLIOGRAPHY

[42] E. Brickell, J. Camenisch, and L. Chen. Direct anonymous attestation. In *CCS '04: Proceedings of the 11th ACM conference on Computer and communications security*, pages 132–145, New York, NY, USA, 2004. ACM.

[43] J. C. Brustoloni, R. Villamarín-Salomón, P. Djalaliev, and D. Kyle. Evaluating the usability of usage controls in electronic collaboration. In *SOUPS '08: Proceedings of the 4th symposium on Usable privacy and security*, pages 85–92, New York, NY, USA, 2008. ACM.

[44] I. Burnett, S. Davis, and G. Drury. MPEG-21 digital item declaration and Identification - principles and compression. *Multimedia, IEEE Transactions on*, 7(3):400–407, June 2005.

[45] I. Burnett, R. Van de Walle, K. Hill, J. Bormans, and F. Pereira. MPEG-21: Goals and Achievements. *IEEE MultiMedia*, 10(4):60–70, 2003.

[46] I. S. Burnett, F. Pereira, R. V. d. Walle, and R. Koenen. *The MPEG-21 Book*. John Wiley & Sons, 2006.

[47] D. Cooper, S. Santesson, S. Farrell, S. Boeyen, R. Housley, and W. Polk. Internet X.509 Public Key Infrastructure - Certificate and Certificate Revocation List (CRL) Profile. Technical Report RFC 5280, The Internet Engineering Task Force (IETF), 2008. http://www.ietf.org/rfc/rfc5280.txt.

[48] K. Diepold, F. Pereira, and W. Chang. MPEG-A: multimedia application formats. *Multimedia, IEEE*, 12(4):34–41, Oct.-Dec. 2005.

[49] T. Dierks and E. Rescorla. The Transport Layer Security (TLS) Protocol. Technical Report RFC 5246, The Internet Engineering Task Force (IETF), 2008. http://tools.ietf.org/html/rfc5246.

[50] D. Eastlake, J. Reagle, D. Solo, F. Hirsch, and T. Roessler. XML Signature Syntax and Processing (Second Edition). Technical report, World Wide Web Consortium (W3C) and The Internet Engineering Task Force (IETF), United States, 2008.

[51] ETSI TS 101 903. *XML Advanced Electronic Signatures (XAdES)*. European Telecommunications Standards Institute (ETSI), 2009.

[52] O. Foundation. *OpenID Authentication 2.0 - Final.* 2007. Available online at http://openid.net/specs/openid-authentication-2_0.html; visited on April 27th 2010. Website [Online].

[53] H. Frederick. XML Signature Properties. Technical report, World Wide Web Consortium (W3C), 2010.

[54] Hyun-Kyung-Oh and Seung-Hun-Jin. The security limitations of SSO in OpenID. In *2008 10th International Conference on Advanced Communication Technology, Gangwon-Do, South Korea, 17-20 Feb. 2008*, pages 1608–1611, Piscataway, NJ, USA, 2008. IEEE.

[55] R. Iannella. *ODRL Creative Commons Profile.* ODRL Initiative, 2005. Available online at http://odrl.net/Profiles/CC/SPEC.html; visited on August 6th 2010. Website [Online].

[56] T. Imamura, B. Dillaway, and E. Simon. XML Encryption Syntax and Processing. Technical report, World Wide Web Consortium (W3C), United States, 2002.

[57] ISO 2108:2005. *Information and documentation - International standard book number (ISBN).* ISO, 2001.

[58] ISO 3901:2001. *Information and documentation - International Standard Recording Code (ISRC).* ISO, 2001.

[59] ISO/IEC 11889-1:2009. *Information technology - Trusted Platform Module - Part 1: Overview.* ISO/IEC, 2009.

[60] ISO/IEC 11889-2:2009. *Information technology - Trusted Platform Module - Part 2: Design principles.* ISO/IEC, 2009.

[61] ISO/IEC 11889-3:2009. *Information technology - Trusted Platform Module - Part 3: Structures.* ISO/IEC, 2009.

[62] ISO/IEC 11889-4:2009. *Information technology - Trusted Platform Module - Part 4: Commands.* ISO/IEC, 2009.

[63] ISO/IEC 14496-12:2005. *Information technology - Coding of audiovisual objects - Part 12: ISO base media file format.* ISO/IEC, 2005.

[64] ISO/IEC 15938-5:2003. *Information technology - Multimedia content description interface (MPEG-7) - Part 5: Multimedia description schemes.* ISO/IEC, 2003.

[65] ISO/IEC 18014-1:2008. *Information technology - Security techniques - Time-stamping services - Part 1: Framework.* ISO/IEC, 2008.

[66] ISO/IEC 18014-2:2009. *Information technology - Security techniques - Time-stamping services - Part 2: Mechanisms producing independent tokens.* ISO/IEC, 2009.

[67] ISO/IEC 18014-3:2009. *Information technology - Security techniques - Time-stamping services - Part 3: Mechanisms producing linked tokens.* ISO/IEC, 2009.

[68] ISO/IEC 21000-1:2004. *Information technology - Multimedia framework (MPEG-21) - Part 1: Vision, Technology and Strategy.* ISO/IEC, 2004.

[69] ISO/IEC 21000-15:2006. *Information technology - Multimedia framework (MPEG-21) - Part 15: Event Reporting.* ISO/IEC, 2006.

[70] ISO/IEC 21000-2:2005. *Information technology - Multimedia framework (MPEG-21) - Part 2: Digital Item Declaration.* ISO/IEC, 2005.

[71] ISO/IEC 21000-3:2003. *Information technology - Multimedia framework (MPEG-21) - Part 3: Digital Item Identification.* ISO/IEC, 2003.

[72] ISO/IEC 21000-3/Amd1:2007. *Information technology - Multimedia framework (MPEG-21) - Part 3: Digital Item Identification, AMENDMENT 1: Relates identifier types.* ISO/IEC, 2007.

[73] ISO/IEC 21000-4:2006. *Information technology - Multimedia framework (MPEG-21) - Part 4: Intellectual Property Management and Protection Components.* ISO/IEC, 2006.

[74] ISO/IEC 21000-5:2004. *Information technology - Multimedia framework (MPEG-21) - Part 5: Rights Expression Language.* ISO/IEC, 2004.

[75] ISO/IEC 21000-5/Amd3:2008. *Information technology - Multimedia framework (MPEG-21) - Part 5: Rights Expression Language, AMENDMENT 3: OAC (Open Access Content) Profile*. ISO/IEC, 2008.

[76] ISO/IEC 21000-6:2004. *Information technology - Multimedia framework (MPEG-21) - Part 6: Rights Data Dictionary*. ISO/IEC, 2004.

[77] ISO/IEC 21000-8/Amd1:2009. *Information technology - Multimedia framework (MPEG-21) - Part 8: Reference software, AMENDMENT 1: Extra reference software*. ISO/IEC, 2009.

[78] ISO/IEC 21000-9:2009. *Information technology - Multimedia framework (MPEG-21) - Part 9: File Format*. ISO/IEC, 2005.

[79] ISO/IEC 23000-5:2008. *Information technology - Multimedia application format (MPEG-A) - Part 5: Media streaming application format*. ISO/IEC, 2008.

[80] ISO/IEC 23000-7:2008. *Information technology - Multimedia application format (MPEG-A) - Part 7: Open access application format*. ISO/IEC, 2008.

[81] ISO/IEC 23000-7/Amd1:2009. *Information technology - Multimedia application format (MPEG-A) - Part 7: Open access application format, AMENDMENT 1: Conformance and reference software for open access application format*. ISO/IEC, 2009.

[82] A. Klenk, H. Kinkelin, C. Eunicke, and G. Carle. Preventing identity theft with electronic identity cards and the trusted platform module. In *EUROSEC '09: Proceedings of the Second European Workshop on System Security*, pages 44–51, New York, NY, USA, 2009. ACM.

[83] G. Klyne and J. J. Carroll. Resource Description Framework (RDF): Concepts and Abstract Syntax. Technical report, World Wide Web Consortium (W3C), 2004.

[84] D. Kyle and J. C. Brustoloni. Uclinux: a linux security module for trusted-computing-based usage controls enforcement. In *STC '07: Proceedings of the 2007 ACM workshop on Scalable trusted computing*, pages 63–70, New York, NY, USA, 2007. ACM.

[85] H. Lee, I. Jeun, K. Chun, and J. Song. A New Anti-phishing Method in OpenID. In *SECURWARE '08: Proceedings of the 2008 Second International Conference on Emerging Security Information, Systems and Technologies*, pages 243–247, Washington, DC, USA, 2008. IEEE Computer Society.

[86] B. Manjunath, P. Salembier, and T. Sikora. *Introduction to MPEG-7: Multimedia Content Description Interface*. John Wiley and Sons, 2002.

[87] J. Martinez, R. Koenen, and F. Pereira. MPEG-7: the generic multimedia content description standard, part 1. *Multimedia, IEEE*, 9(2):78–87, apr-jun 2002.

[88] Open Mobile Alliance. *DRM Rights Expression Language*. 2008. Available online at http://www.openmobilealliance.org/Technical/release_program/docs/DRM/V2_1-20081106-A/OMA-TS-DRM_REL-V2_1-20081014-A.pdf; visited on August 4th 2010. Website [Online].

[89] D. Recordon and D. Reed. OpenID 2.0: a platform for user-centric identity management. In *DIM '06: Proceedings of the second ACM workshop on Digital identity management*, pages 11–16, New York, NY, USA, 2006. ACM.

[90] D. Reed and D. McAlpin. Extensible Resource Identifier (XRI) Syntax V2.0. Technical report, Organization for the Advancement of Structured Information Standards (OASIS), 2005.

[91] E. Rodriguez and J. Delgado. Towards the Interoperability between MPEG-21 REL and Creative Commons Licenses. In *Automated Production of Cross Media Content for Multi-Channel Distribution, 2006. AXMEDIS '06. Second International Conference on*, pages 45–52, Washington, DC, USA, Dec. 2006. IEEE Computer Society.

[92] E. Rodriguez, I. Gallego, and J. Delgado. Use of MPEG-21 for License Protection and Key Management in DRM Systems. In *AXMEDIS '07: Proceedings of the Third International Conference on Automated Production of Cross Media Content for Multi-Channel Distribution*, pages 163–170, Washington, DC, USA, 2007. IEEE Computer Society.

[93] A.-R. Sadeghi, M. Selhorst, C. Stüble, C. Wachsmann, and M. Winandy. TCG inside?: a note on TPM specification compliance. In *STC '06: Proceedings of the first ACM workshop on Scalable trusted computing*, pages 47–56, New York, NY, USA, 2006. ACM.

[94] P. Salembier and J. Smith. MPEG-7 multimedia description schemes. *Circuits and Systems for Video Technology, IEEE Transactions on*, 11(6):748 –759, jun 2001.

[95] D. Schellekens, B. Wyseur, and B. Preneel. Remote attestation on legacy operating systems with trusted platform modules. *Sci. Comput. Program.*, 74(1-2):13–22, 2008.

[96] F. Schreiner and K. Diepold. *MPEG-A and its Open Access Application Format*. The Handbook of MPEG Applications: Standards in Practice. John Wiley & Sons, 2010.

[97] F. Schreiner, K. Diepold, M. Abo El-Fotouh, and T. Kim. Standards: The MPEG Open Access Application Format. *Multimedia, IEEE*, 16(3):8–12, July-Sept. 2009.

[98] N. P. Sheppard. On implementing mpeg-21 intellectual property management and protection. In *DRM '07: Proceedings of the 2007 ACM workshop on Digital Rights Management*, pages 10–22, New York, NY, USA, 2007. ACM.

[99] S. Stamm, N. P. Sheppard, and R. Safavi-Naini. Implementing Trusted Terminals with a and SITDRM. *Electron. Notes Theor. Comput. Sci.*, 197(1):73–85, 2008.

[100] F. Stumpf, A. Fuchs, S. Katzenbeisser, and C. Eckert. Improving the scalability of platform attestation. In *STC '08: Proceedings of the 3rd ACM workshop on Scalable trusted computing*, pages 1–10, New York, NY, USA, 2008. ACM.

[101] A. Tokmakoff, F.-X. Nuttall, and K. Ji. MPEG-21 Event Reporting: Enabling Multimedia E-Commerce. *IEEE MultiMedia*, 12(4):50–59, 2005.

[102] Trusted Computing Group. *TCG Software Stack (TSS) Specification*. 2007. Available online at http://www.trustedcomputinggroup.org/

files/resource_files/6479CD77-1D09-3519-AD89EAD1BC8C97F0/TSS\
_1_2_Errata_A-final.pdf; visited on April 22th 2010. Website
[Online].

[103] Trusted Computing Group. *TPM Main Specification - Part 1 Design Principles*. 2007. Available online at http://www.trustedcomputinggroup.org/files/resource_files/ACD19914-1D09-3519-ADA64741A1A15795/mainP1DPrev103.zip; visited on April 17th 2010. Website [Online].

[104] Trusted Computing Group. *TPM Main Specification - Part 2 TPM Structures*. 2007. Available online at http://www.trustedcomputinggroup.org/files/resource_files/E14876A3-1A4B-B294-D086297A1ED38F96/mainP2Structrev103.pdf; visited on April 17th 2010. Website [Online].

[105] Trusted Computing Group. *TPM Main Specification - Part 3 Commands*. 2007. Available online at http://www.trustedcomputinggroup.org/files/resource_files/E14A09AD-1A4B-B294-D049ACC1A1A138ED/mainP3Commandsrev103.pdf; visited on April 17th 2010. Website [Online].

[106] G. Wachob and D. Reed. Extensible Resource Identifier (XRI) Resolution Version 2.0. Technical report, Organization for the Advancement of Structured Information Standards (OASIS), 2008.

[107] X. Wang, T. DeMartini, B. Wragg, M. Paramasivam, and C. Barlas. The MPEG-21 rights expression language and rights data dictionary. *Multimedia, IEEE Transactions on*, 7(3):408–417, June 2005.

[108] K. Wouters, B. Preneel, A. I. González-Tablas, and A. Ribagorda. Towards an XML format for time-stamps. In *XMLSEC '02: Proceedings of the 2002 ACM workshop on XML security*, pages 61–70, New York, NY, USA, 2002. ACM.

List of Figures

2.1	Basic scenario for the file format and metadata	31
2.2	Hierarchical structure of the standards within a file	33
2.3	Structure of the rights expressions	38
2.4	Example of adaptation and relationships	42
2.5	Hierarchy of relationships between derived Items	43
2.6	Full scenario of the file format and metadata	44
2.7	Hierarchical structure of the file format	46
3.1	Syntax of the *EncryptedKey* element	50
3.2	Structure of a XML signature	52
3.3	Creation of a qualified timestamp according to the Time-Stamp Protocol	54
3.4	Structure of the GenericTimeStampType	56
3.5	Tick counter and its output	61
3.6	Creation of a tickstamp	62
3.7	Timestamp protocol sequence	63
3.8	OpenID redirect protocol	67
3.9	Encapsulated signature within an Item	82
3.10	Content encryption with MPEG-21 IPMP	84
3.11	Method for key exchange within an Item	86
3.12	Embedding of a key in an *Annotation* element	89

LIST OF FIGURES

3.13 Timestamp created by the TPM 93
3.14 The GenericTimeStampExtensionType 94
3.15 The *TPMTimeStampType* and its mapping to the TPM-timestamp 95
3.16 The *TickStampType* and its mapping to the tickstamp 96
3.17 Example of integration in XMLDSig 98
3.18 Example of a XMLDSig signature with a TPM-timestamp . . 99
3.19 Overview of the OpenID system with the TPM 101
3.20 Registration of a user at the Provider 105
3.21 Authentication protocol 107

4.1 Overview of the system components 114
4.2 Architecture of the Content Management Application 116
4.3 Main window of the Content Management Application 118
4.4 User interface of the Content Server in a browser 125
4.5 Architecture of the browser add-on and its connections 128

i want morebooks!

Buy your books fast and straightforward online - at one of world's fastest growing online book stores! Environmentally sound due to Print-on-Demand technologies.

Buy your books online at
www.get-morebooks.com

Kaufen Sie Ihre Bücher schnell und unkompliziert online – auf einer der am schnellsten wachsenden Buchhandelsplattformen weltweit! Dank Print-On-Demand umwelt- und ressourcenschonend produziert.

Bücher schneller online kaufen
www.morebooks.de

VDM Verlagsservicegesellschaft mbH
Heinrich-Böcking-Str. 6-8   Telefon: +49 681 3720 174   info@vdm-vsg.de
D - 66121 Saarbrücken   Telefax: +49 681 3720 1749   www.vdm-vsg.de

Printed by Books on Demand GmbH, Norderstedt / Germany